# Daughter of Fortune

## *The Bettie Brown Story*

Sherrie S. McLeRoy

REPUBLIC OF TEXAS PRESS
*Lanham • Boulder • New York • Toronto • Oxford*

Published by Republic of Texas Press
An imprint of The Rowman & Littlefield Publishing Group, Inc.
4501 Forbes Boulevard, Suite 200
Lanham, MD 20706

Distributed by NATIONAL BOOK NETWORK

**Library of Congress Cataloging-in-Publication Data**

McLeRoy, Sherrie S.
    Daughter of fortune: the Bettie Brown story / by Sherrie S. McLeRoy.
        p.  cm.—(Women of the West series)
    Includes bibliographical references and index.
    ISBN 1-55622-529-6
    1. Brown, Bettie. 2. Socialites—Texas—Galveston—Biography.
    3. Galveston (Tex.)—Biography. I. Title. II. Series.
F394.G2M38   1996
976.4'139—dc20                       96-23324

Manufactured in the United States of America.

To the memory of
Judy D. Schiebel,
first administrator of
Ashton Villa House Museum,
and
to the other "Steel Oleanders"
who have helped to build Galveston.

# Contents

Contents

# List of Illustrations

# Introduction

I actually began this book twelve years ago.

I had spent a year and a half (1982-1983) working at Texas' *Ashton Villa* House Museum, where I was the first professional curator on the staff of the Galveston Historical Foundation (GHF), which operates the mansion. My boss was a short, red-going-grey-haired dynamo named Judy D. Schiebel, who had been the *Ashton Villa* administrator since the museum opened in 1974 and who was the acknowledged and legendary master of "dog and pony shows" in Texas museum circles.

Now, it's a funny thing about working in museums (which I did for more than fifteen years). You can get so lost in the minutiae of administration and endless special events and busloads of tourists who show up for a tour without a reservation that you sometimes lose sight of what—and who—it is you're trying to interpret. Like most of the curators who have followed me, I was simply too busy to do much additional digging and research on the Browns; I relied on the excellent history and oral interviews put together by *Ashton Villa's* first chairman, Inez Lasall. Only after I left to work at another GHF project, the *1839 Williams Home*, did I begin to poke around with the intention of doing a magazine article about *Ashton Villa's* most famous inhabitant, Rebecca Ashton Brown, a.k.a. Miss Bettie.

I'm from Virginia, and I love that place and its history dearly. But I can still state, without hesitation or equivocation, that Texas has grown some of the damnedest women I have ever run across. They're bold, they're free spirited, and they do not give a toot whether society is frowning on their ways or not. To me, Bettie Brown was the personification of that Texas woman.

So I started digging but got busy with first one job and then another, and then a move to Sherman, Texas. And a new job. And, finally, a new career as a writer. It was not until last year, when I finished *Red River Women* for Republic of Texas Press' "Women of the West" series, that I had the leisure to look about and wonder what I would write on next. Bettie came to mind, and I scrambled around in boxes to find my old notes.

When I approached the Galveston Historical Foundation about the project, Betty Massey, my old colleague who is now executive director of GHF, was instantly excited. It seemed that 1996 would mark GHF's 125th anniversary, and the publication of a first-ever biography of Bettie would be a perfect way to end the year. So I started working in earnest, wondering for a few panic-stricken minutes how I would make a book of Galveston's perennial party girl.

But to my surprise, I found Bettie. The real Bettie. The one we've been pretty much missing all these years, who was hidden behind the expensively coiffed and gowned and jeweled Bettie. The woman whom life and turmoil changed—surprise! —just as it does most of us.

What I discovered was that Bettie was a unique woman at a unique time for all women, a crucial period when the mores and strictures that had bound them for most of the so-called Victorian period were giving way to the stresses and the turmoil and the mind-boggling technical achievements that marked the early twentieth century. Many of the inventions and social customs that you and I take for granted today—everything from the elevator to the telephone to the country club—were products of the late Victorian period. And they, along with fantastic new communications and transportation systems, were changing our world, opening it in a way never before seen.

Some women (and some men, for that matter) never made the leap to this brave new world. But Bettie Brown did, jumping in with both feet, for she had learned the secret and importance of adaptability from her father. She was the forerunner of what historians would later call the "modern woman," who emerged about the time of World War I. And though Bettie never actually worked for a salary—the hallmark of this modern damsel—she invested her time and energy and executive ability in volunteer positions just as surely as if she had.

She never married, never surrendered control of her property and her very body to a man. That was not to say she didn't enjoy a long line of admirers, perhaps even lovers. I would have given a great deal to have found some of Bettie's love letters, but she was too discreet, despite the reputation she had.

And about that reputation. Everyone who's been through *Ashton Villa* or heard stories about Bettie believes that she led a somewhat sordid life. After looking at the evidence, I think most of those tales were made up by one or two enemies who spread them very well. And Miss Rebecca Ashton Brown, proud daughter of J. M. Brown, would never have deigned to even recognize that the stories existed, let alone refute them. Did she laugh about them, the rumors and the "honest to God true stories," in private? Or did they hurt? Perhaps it hurt more just that they *were* believed.

I've come to admire Bettie in the months of working on this book. I wish I could have answered all the questions I had about her, but those answers will have to wait. I've researched every place I could think of in an effort to tell her real story, but the elusive letters and diaries that would have filled in the remaining few holes either don't exist or haven't come to light yet.

I couldn't have written *Daughter of Fortune* without a lot of help from several people. Beth Weidler, GHF's curator for both *Ashton Villa* and the *Williams Home*, took pictures, dragged out boxes of records, answered questions, read the draft of this book for mistakes (those that remain are my own), and eagerly discussed all my findings and revelations. Anna Peebler, archivist at the Galveston-Texas History Center of the

Rosenberg Library, was equally super about tracking down elusive information and answering panicked inquiries over the phone. ("Just *who* was so and so?!")

Margaret Doran at the Moody Mansion and Museum brought Colonel W. L. Moody's marvelous 1902 diary to me: never will I forget sitting in my hotel room and reading it through until two in the morning, howling with laughter over the Colonel's pungent wit and his description of Miss Bettie riding a camel. And my thanks to another longtime friend, Betty Massey, executive director of GHF, who endorsed this project and helped make it work.

My deepest thanks go to several descendants of J. M. Brown, who have gladly shared their knowledge of the family with *Ashton Villa* staff through the years and with me: Mrs. Henry J. Jumonville Jr. of New Orleans; Mr. J. M. Brown III of San Francisco; Mrs. T. J. Stanly of Nacogdoches, Texas; Mr. Albert Ball of Sealy, Texas; and Mrs. Michael Doherty of Galveston. They and other family members have helped bring *Ashton Villa* back to life.

Thanks to my editor, Mary Elizabeth Goldman, who thinks that books about women are *interesting* and worth writing.

And, as always, thanks to my husband Bill, who not only lives with a writer but encourages me to do more. He'll probably blanch, but I hope our daughter, Ann Elizabeth, grows up to have a bit of Bettie Brown's spunk and *savoir faire*.

And lastly, I say thank you to Bettie herself. She and other women like her led the way and made it possible for Texas women like me to pursue our careers without (too much) prejudice—to write books or drive forklifts or fly through space . . . whatever our hearts desire and can dream.

Sherrie S. McLeRoy

# Descended from the Lords of Wales

Bettie's maternal ancestry traces back to ancient Wales, a mountainous region that plagued England for generations with its fierce spirit of independence. Centuries before Edward I conquered Wales and made it part of the crown's holdings in 1284, the earliest of Bettie's known ancestors had settled in the area of Brecon, a town located some thirty-five miles northwest of Cardiff on the edge of the Brecon Beacons, red sandstone peaks in the wild heart of South Wales.

## WELSH ANCESTRY

In his classic work *Colonial Families of Philadelphia*, John W. Jordan traced the first Powels back through "the mists" to one Gorwst Ledlwn, "a British chieftain or regulus in Cumbria [*sic*]," that is, Wales. (For genealogy chart, see Appendix B.) One descendant of his was Rhodri Mawr, crowned king of all Wales in 843. Then there was Gwallawg, "pendragon" or king of northern Britain, and Teithwalch, who defeated Aethelbald, the Earl of Mercia in 728.

1

Bleddyn ap* Maenarch, the Lord of Brecknock (as Brecon County was originally called, in honor of a Powel ancestor), married Oten, the sister of Rhys ap Tewdwr, the Prince of South Wales. But Bleddyn died at Caerbannan in 1091, along with his brother-in-law, when Normans overran the region—the so-called marcher lords—and ended its ancient British rule.

Eight generations later, Bleddyn's descendant Sir David (Dafyd) Gam fell at the Battle of Agincourt in 1415 after an adventurous career that included being held for ransom by Welsh activist Owen Glendower. Five more generations would pass before another of Bleddyn's descendants, Thomas ap Howel, changed the family name to Powel, a corruption or Anglicization of "ap Howel" and the name by which the rest of this line was called. The Powel motto was "Death before dishonor," and the crest included a lion rampant and a wyvern, a fantastic winged creature which stood on two legs and had the head of a dragon.[1]

## CASTLE MADOC

When Thomas ap Howel, Bleddyn's descendant, built *Castle Madoc* in 1580, he probably named the structure in honor of ancestor Madoc, the third son of Dafyd ap Rhys-y-ddimau. With wife Margaret Vaughan, Thomas built on the site of an older "castellated mansion, with a keep for prisoners upon an artificial mound," midway between modern Brecon and Builth Wells, to the north.[2] It remained in the Powel family more than 200 years before passing out of the direct line to a cousin. Among the Powels who lived there were several High Sheriffs of Breconshire and a poet, William Powel, son of the builder.

---

\*     "ap" means son of.

## TO AMERICA

Sometime around 1730 or 1740, the first Powel crossed the Atlantic to settle in Philadelphia. William Powel (1684-1754) was the second of seven children of Charles and Elizabeth Powel. To his older brother Hugh would go *Castle Madoc*; William received only £95 from his father with which to establish himself and his wife, another Elizabeth, in America.[3]

His son William (?-1757) married Sarah Mifflin (1718-1795) of a prominent Quaker family which had emigrated from Warminster, England to Pennsylvania about 1676. John Mifflin Sr. (1638-1716), Sarah's great-grandfather, and his son John Jr. settled on the Delaware River among Swedish colonists before building *Fountain Green* on a land grant from the Duke of York. Sarah's brother John would father one of Pennsylvania's best known Revolutionary figures, Major General and later Governor Thomas Mifflin;[4] and William and Sarah themselves had six sons before their only daughter, Rebecca, was born.

It was Rebecca Powel (1741-1809) who would forge the next link to a name that loomed large in Bettie Brown's life.[5] At the age of twenty-six, Rebecca married Isaac Ashton (1742-1777) in Philadelphia's historic Christ Church (built in 1727).

## THE ASHTONS

The Ashtons of Philadelphia descended from the Assheton family of Ashton(Assheton)-Under-Lyne, today part of the sprawling Greater Manchester metroplex. That line dates back to the thirteenth century and later includes such notables as Sir Robert de Assheton, Lord Treasurer of England (1363), Treasurer of the Exchequer (1373), and Warden of the Cinque Ports (1381), as well as Sir John de Assheton, considered one of the most influential nobles of his time and a knight of the Order of Bath (1399).

Jonathan Assheton was the first of the family to reach Philadelphia in 1683, where he became clerk of Christ Church (Church of England). Isaac Ashton, who would become Bettie's forebear, was probably his grandson.[6]

Very little is known about this young man. Isaac was born in Philadelphia in 1742 and married Rebecca Powel twenty-five years later. During the Revolutionary War, he rose to the rank of Second Lieutenant of Artillery and served in Captain Samuel Massey's company of Colonel Jehu Eyre's Battalion along with his brother-in-law Samuel Powel (1739-1814). Isaac was killed in the conflict on September 7, 1777, possibly in some of the fighting that led up to the British capture of Philadelphia on September 26; the records are very unclear.

But his impact on Bettie Brown's life would be an immense one, considering Isaac's short life of only thirty-five years. Four of the next five generations of his descendants would include a "Rebecca Ashton"—like Bettie—and Bettie's Galveston home would bear the name of this ancestor.

Rebecca and Isaac Ashton had three daughters, among them Bettie's great-grandmother Rebecca.[7] Born less than two months after her father's death, this Rebecca (1777-1869) also grew up in Philadelphia and, in 1798, married John Stoddart, the English-born son of Henry and Ann Stoddart. The Stoddarts had thirteen children, all but two of whom lived to adulthood.[8]

## JOHN STODDART

John was considered one of Philadelphia's outstanding businessmen, whose every venture was a success. He and Rebecca had a "palatial residence" at the corner of Seventh and Race streets, facing Franklin Square and filled with the finest furniture imported from England. (It was demolished about 1920.)

John acquired thousands of acres of land in the Wilkes-Barre region of Pennsylvania and established the town of Stoddartsville on what was to be the route of the Lehigh Navigation Company's canal. But the project never materialized and the town dwindled, although second son Isaac Ashton Stoddart, named for his maternal grandfather, supervised the estate for many years.

John continued to be active in several businesses, including dry-goods and book publishing, but then unwisely assigned "all his property for the benefit of his creditors, amounting to the sum of $600,000. . . ." The money was lost. After this debacle, John and Rebecca left their spacious townhouse and moved back to the small house on North Seventh Street, next to the synagogue, where she had been born in 1777.[9]

Their fourth son, another John Stoddart, was an agent for the New York Coal Company and married Sarah Warner Moses (1806-1903), whose background is almost as elusive as Isaac Ashton's. According to Annie Doom Pickrell, author of *Pioneer Women of Texas*, the half-Jewish Sarah was shunned by her father-in-law because of her ethnic background.[10] Sarah, wrote Pickrell, quarreled bitterly with the Stoddarts and thereafter refused to have anything to do with them. Her two daughters, Matilda Ella and Rebecca Ashton, visited their father's family without her.

The problem lies in the many other fallacies in Pickrell's account—the only biography of Sarah's early life—which cast doubts on the accuracy of the whole. Was Sarah, in fact, Jewish? And did that color her relationship with her in-laws?

## GONE TO TEXAS

When John Stoddart died in 1833 at the young age of twenty-eight, Sarah stayed on in Philadelphia for some time before deciding to leave and move her family south to the

Mexican state of Coahuila and Texas. Why? Pickrell wrote that friends of Sarah's had sent her favorable reports of the country there; but was she also influenced by the sizeable Jewish population that had settled in the port city of Galveston? Or did Sarah decide to scratch "Gone to Texas" on her door, as so many others were doing, and seek a new life there?

Even the date of her departure from Philadelphia is in question. Family legend places it about 1833, but there was very little in the way of settlements in Galveston at that time. Shipping records are virtually nonexistent from this period, so she cannot be traced in that manner. Kenneth Hafertepe, author of *A History of Ashton Villa* (1991), states the family arrived in the mid 1840s. For the purposes of this account, a date that falls somewhere between the two will be considered the correct one.[11]

On the voyage down the Atlantic coast and across the Gulf of Mexico, Sarah, who was described as the prettiest woman in Philadelphia by her contemporaries, met a hardware merchant from Rhode Island named Charles K. Rhodes (1807-circa 1893), on his way to set up a new business in Galveston. They fell in love and were probably married after they reached Galveston, and they raised her two Stoddart daughters, Matilda and Rebecca, there. One descendant says that Sarah managed and/or owned a hotel "down the Island," *i.e.*, in the modern West End, and regularly drove a team of mules into town.

Rebecca Ashton Stoddart Brown (1831-1907), Bettie's mother, descended from a prominent Philadelphia family. Her daughters Bettie and Matilda inherited her "Stoddart" nose. (Circa 1890) (Courtesy *Ashton Villa*)

## GROWING UP IN GALVESTON

The younger of Sarah's girls, Rebecca Ashton Stoddart had been born in Philadelphia on November 18, 1831 and was said to have been only two or so when the family emigrated to Texas. And the Galveston that she grew up in was far different from the "Victorian" landscape that today's visitors see.

The city of Galveston is located at the eastern tip of a long, thin island of the same name, both called in honor of the Conde de Galvez (1746-1786), Spanish governor of Louisiana who ordered one of the earliest surveys of what would be Galveston Bay. First explored by Europeans in the sixteenth century, the island, which separates the Bay from the Gulf of Mexico, was not settled by them until the early and mid-1820s. For several more decades, it remained unconnected to the Texas mainland and accessible only by boat.

Still, Galveston grew quickly, thanks to its strategic location and natural, though shallow, harbor; shipping lines soon connected it with New Orleans and the fledgling town of Houston. When war broke out late in 1835 between Texas and Mexico, Galveston flourished as supplies and recruits poured in. But after Mexican general Antonio Lopez de Santa Anna sent his armies north to plunder, burn, and kill, the town also filled with refugees hoping to flee the conflict and return to the United States: the infamous Runaway Scrape. Among those who sought sanctuary were the officers of Texas' first government, formed when the colony declared independence on March 2, 1836.

The Galveston of Rebecca Stoddart's childhood was a village of low frame houses built around the harbor (some on posts to escape high tide), of stores built so close to the water that one could fish out the back door, and great excitement at the arrival of every vessel, bringing news of the outside world. Soon after the war with Mexico, the town's size and population both accelerated as Texans began shipping their white gold—cotton—through its port facilities. Cotton would make Galveston not only Texas' largest city in only a few years, but its cultural and commercial heart as well.

## ENTER MR. BROWN

Which is precisely what attracted a young New Yorker by the name of James Moreau Brown.

Little is known of his ancestry. His obituary states that he was the son of Dutch immigrants, but histories of Orange County, New York, where Brown was born on September 22, 1821, describe his unnamed grandfather as an Englishman who settled in the Cornwall area of that county prior to the Revolutionary War.

The family's own questions about this side of their ancestry center around James Brown's middle name. "Moreau" is an old French term for a dark-haired or dark-skinned person. It is also the name of one of Napoleon's generals, who, according to family history, visited the Brown home in New York on his American trip sometime prior to James Brown's birth. Possibly James' English-born grandfather was the son of a French mother who provided the connection to that country. The records are regrettably unclear in explaining this mystery.

Cornwall, James Brown's birthplace, is a picturesque town on the Hudson River in what is known as "the Highlands of the Hudson" and, in the nineteenth century, included the U.S. Military Academy at West Point in its bounds. It was first settled by the Dutch, followed by French Huguenots and English in the eighteenth century. Here the unknown Mr. Brown from England raised six children, among them James' father John Brown.[12]

John, a Cornwall farmer, married Hannah Cronk (Krountz, Kratz), who was undoubtedly of the locale's early Dutch heritage.[13] They had sixteen children, ten of whom lived to adulthood: Ann, William S., Henry, Edward, John, Hedges, James

Moreau, Elliott, Louisa, and Esther. One of his biographers wrote that the family moved to New York City when James was a child, but the author was unable to confirm this.

By all accounts, the Browns were at least moderately well off, and James received some formal education. But he was an adventurous youth and made his first escape from home and family at the age of twelve. Two years passed before his family found him. He soon left again, this time for the western part of the state and a job "driving" boats on the Erie Canal. There, he is alleged to have met and become friends, possibly even business partners for a time, with Charles Mallory, who would later found one of the first large steamship lines servicing Galveston.

When he finally returned home, his father apprenticed James to a brickmason and plasterer. He completed his term of service, then left for the last time about 1838, journeying through the South and along the Ohio River to build courthouses, cisterns, and jails in growing towns.[14] He stopped in New Orleans, then in Vicksburg, Mississippi for a time, where he is said to have begun accumulating wealth and property before moving on to Texas and Galveston sometime in the early 1840s.

Brown's obituary gives his arrival date as 1842 or 1843, but research conducted by Kenneth Hafertepe turned up no documentary evidence of his presence before 1846. Hafertepe speculates that, contrary to the stories that James Brown owned the company that built the first brick structures in Galveston, he likely worked as someone else's employee before discarding brickmasonry to go into the hardware business with Henry H. Brower in 1847. They built their store, Brown & Brower Hardware, on Market Street but remained partners only a year before James bought out Brower's interest.

James Moreau Brown (1821-1895) was Bettie's father and built *Ashton Villa*. He is considered one of the most influential business personalities of Victorian Galveston. (Circa 1890.) (Courtesy *Ashton Villa*)

## MARRIAGE AND FAMILY

By that time, James had married Sarah Stoddart Rhodes' youngest daughter, sixteen-year-old Rebecca Ashton Rhodes, as she is titled in their license. (Her older sister Matilda had already married Henry Garlic(k) a year earlier on January 12, 1847.)[15] They likely met while attending services at Trinity Episcopal Church where they were married on April 9, 1848 by the church's founding rector, Benjamin Eaton. In December, Rebecca gave birth to the first of their five children, John Stoddart, named for John Brown and John Stoddart, the father Rebecca had barely known.

James built a new wooden structure on Market Street to house both his hardware store and, on the upper floor, his family. His business was flourishing and, despite his comparatively young age of twenty-seven, he was "thorough, methodical and systematic in everything he undertook" and had already gained enough respect in Galveston to be elected an alderman on the City Council.[16] In 1850 he took on a new partner, Stephen Kirkland, another New Yorker, and they relocated the store to The Strand, Galveston's main business street. Two years after second son Moreau Roberts was born in 1853, Brown & Kirkland expanded even more by erecting a magnificent, three-story brick building at a new site on The Strand. Next door, James opened a second business, J. M. Brown's Carriage Repository, which he owned with another partner.

By the time the fourth Rebecca Ashton of her line was born in the Market Street house on February 18, 1855, her father was fast on his way to becoming one of Galveston's premier citizens. Such a position, coupled with a growing family, dictated James Brown's next move: the building of *Ashton Villa*, the home in which his elder daughter, nicknamed Bettie, would live the rest of her life.

## Notes: Chapter One

1   Information for this section from *Annals and Antiquities of the Counties and County Families of Wales* (1872) by Thomas Nicholas and from *Colonial Families of Philadelphia* (1911) by John W. Jordan.

2   The site still appears on maps of Wales as Castle Madoc, on the B4520 highway. The author was unable to confirm whether the structure still exists.

3   The exact relationship between Bettie's ancestral Powels and Samuel Powel, "the rich carpenter," is unclear. A Quaker himself, Samuel I amassed an amazing fortune. At the time of his death in 1756, he owned more than 90 houses in Philadelphia and a vast amount of real estate. His grandson, Samuel III, made the Grand Tour of Europe in the 1760s, returning to Philadelphia in 1767 and marrying Elizabeth Willing two years later. Samuel III built a grand townhouse at 244 South Third Street that was the talk of Philadelphia for the lavishness of its furnishings, many of them brought back from Europe. Powel was also a patron of the painter Benjamin West, "the American Raphael," who painted his portrait.

4   Sarah and John Mifflin were the children of Philadelphia merchant George Mifflin (1688-?), a member of the city's Common Council from 1730 until 1757, and of his wife, Esther Cordery, daughter of a Philadelphia pulley-maker.

John Mifflin married twice: (1) Elizabeth Bagnall of Boston, who bore him the above-mentioned Thomas (1744-1800) and George Mifflin (1746-1785), and (2) Sarah Fishburne.

Thomas Mifflin, a Quaker, embarked on the "Grand Tour" of Europe at age twenty-one, as did many other prominent Philadelphia Quakers. During the Revolutionary War, he quickly rose to the rank of major-general but sullied his record by taking part in the Conway Cabal, a plot to replace George Washington as Commander-in-Chief with General Gates. Thomas was elected to Congress in 1783 and was a member of the Constitutional Convention that drafted the federal constitution. His home, *Fort Hill*, was just above the falls of the Schuylkill. John Singleton Copley's portrait of Thomas and his wife is considered one of the best executed in this country during the colonial period.

Thomas' brother George Mifflin was paymaster of the 5th Pennsylvania Battalion during the war.

5   William and Sarah's other child was Samuel Powel (1739-1814) who married (1) Elizabeth Moulder and (2) Elizabeth Coffin(g).

6   Information on the Ashtons from *Colonial Families of Philadelphia* by John W. Jordan (1911), Volume 1, pages 1129-1132.

7   Rebecca and Isaac Ashton's other children were Susan, who married Joseph Marshall; Eleanor, who married Ezekiel Howell; and son Stephen, who died in infancy.

8   Children of Rebecca Ashton and John Stoddart: Henry (1799-1832), Isaac Ashton (1801-1854), Armat (1803-1833, who married one of his mother's Powel cousins), John (1805-1833), Ashton I (1806-1812), Curwen (1809-1890), Ashton II (1810-1810), Rebecca Ann (1813-1836), Martha (1814-1876), Joseph M. (1816-?), Mary Powel (1818-?), Eleanor (1819-?), and Sarah W. (1820-1890).

9   Information on John Stoddart from *Annals of Philadelphia, and Pennsylvania, in the Olden Time* by John F. Watson, Volume 3, pages 450-451.

10   Pickrell also wrote that Sarah Moses Stoddart was the great-granddaughter of "Baron Rhinestein who lived in Castle Rhinestein on the Rhine River, a man of importance in his day in Germany." (Pickrell, page 274)

According to the 1900 Census, Sarah's father was born in Germany and her mother in England.

11    The author's decision on this arrival date is based upon the fact that no marriage record exists in Galveston County records for Sarah Stoddart and C. K. Rhodes (see following paragraph of text). That could indicate they were married on board ship but more likely means the record is to be found somewhere in the Mexican archives, giving it a pre-1836 date.

12    John Brown's siblings included William, Thomas Nathaniel, Frank, Amelia (who married Martin Hallock), and Ann (who married Edward Coffee).

Some sources state James Moreau Brown was born in New York City, but the best available evidence indicates Orange County.

William S. Brown is the only one of James' siblings about whom there is much information. According to *History of Orange County, New York*, he was born in Cornwall, New York in 1809 and received a minimal education. At fifteen, he apprenticed to John Golow of New Windsor "to learn the trade of dressing deer-hides for buckskin." He worked in New York City for eight or nine years as a carter, then at a limekiln in Brooklyn. William moved to Rockland, Maine where he manufactured lime for fourteen years. After another seven years in a New York brokerage and commission house, he returned to Cornwall and took up farming. William married Martha Rose (1807-1876) of Flatbush in 1830 and was the father of seven children.

13    Hannah likely descended from Cornelius Swim, the first settler of Highland Falls in Orange County. According to Russell Headley's *History of Orange County, New York*, "the Swim family had removed to this country from England about the year 1686." One of Swim's granddaughters married into the Dutch Cronk family.

14 Brown's obituary refers to the "diary" he kept of these travels. Unfortunately, it no longer exists.

15 This is probably the same Henry Garlick of Galveston County who received 320 acres from the Republic of Texas in 1839. He and Matilda had four children: William, Henry, Sarah (Sallie) who married Albert Ferrier, and Rebekah.

16 Obituary of James Moreau Brown, *Galveston Daily News*, December 26, 1895.

CHAPTER TWO

# Growing Up in Ashton Villa

In 1859, when Bettie turned four years old, her father became president of the Galveston, Houston and Henderson Railroad, chartered in 1853. J. M. Brown's immediate project was the completion of the line's bridge across Galveston Bay, which connected the island and the mainland for the first time. He would continue as GH&H's president through the Civil War.

Also in 1859, James bought four lots on what was then the outskirts of Galveston, an unfashionable boulevard named Broadway, between 23rd and 24th streets. There he began to build "the first of the great palaces of Galveston," an imposing brick residence in the modern Italianate style which stood head and shoulders above the mostly wooden Galveston.[1]

## ASHTON VILLA

The original structure, as opposed to today's *Ashton Villa*, was square and symmetrical in design, typical of public buildings rather than residences in the Italianate style. Three stories tall, it featured the first cast-iron galleries on any Galveston house, and wooden brackets supporting the overhanging roof. Floor-to-ceiling windows aided circulation in coastal heat and

James Brown completed *Ashton Villa* in 1859 and named it for his wife's Revolutionary War ancestor, Isaac Ashton. This view, circa 1865, shows the original symmetrical block of the house before the east wing was added. Just behind it is the separate kitchen. (Courtesy of Rosenberg Library, Galveston, Texas)

humidity, and a separate brick structure behind the house contained the kitchen, laundry, and slaves/servants' quarters. A third building housed the stable.[2]

To the left, as guests entered the front door of *Ashton Villa*, was a large parlour or reception room that extended the depth of the house. Across the hall was a small "ladies" parlour and, behind it, a dining room. The Browns chose the sophisticated and popular French Antique style to decorate these public rooms: antique reproduction furniture selected and purchased in New York, tall pier mirrors, and an ornate plaster cornice in a floral motif.

Upstairs were several bedrooms with the latest in modern conveniences. Each had a built-in closet and either a half or full bathroom—the first indoor plumbing in the city. Bedrooms for the Brown boys were on the third floor. Coal fireplaces supplemented the gas furnace in the basement, and several large copper and wood cisterns supplied running water.[3] A fairly modest number of slaves, no more than three or four, supported the household.[4]

It was, to say the least, the finest house in Galveston and one of the most impressive and costly in all of Texas. Even the Governor's Mansion in Austin cost no more than the $18,000 J. M. Brown invested in *Ashton Villa*.[5]

He sold the house on Market Street, and the family moved into *Ashton Villa*—christened for Mrs. Brown's Revolutionary War ancestor—in time to host a party on New Year's Day, 1860. But they had little time in which to enjoy it.

## CIVIL WAR

By 1860 Galveston was a bustling city of more than 7,000 people with extensive commercial ties to the rest of the United States and Europe. It had the first newspaper in the state, the longest bridge in the country (Mr. Brown's GH&H bridge across the Bay), the first private bank and telegraph office in the state, and a very firm belief that it was indeed "the Queen City of the Gulf."

And like most of the rest of Texas, its residents voted to secede the state from the Union in February of 1861. Their dismay at discovering the Union had no intention of letting them leave peacefully was quickly followed by a scramble to defend Texas' largest port and one of the most important in the new Confederacy.

But to no avail. A federal blockade soon made life in Galveston very risky, for the navy "had a habit of throwing shells into the town at times, which made it not only an unpleasant but a dangerous place to live."[6] Many people left the island for mainland refuges.

Brown descendants assert that Mrs. Brown and the children, John, Moreau, and Bettie, did likewise, fleeing to Houston. Because of the scarcity of records, this cannot be confirmed, though it certainly would have been prudent. If true, then Bettie would have started her schooling in that city, probably at a private "dame" academy. Soon after the start of the war, James and Rebecca sent oldest son John Stoddart, just becoming a teenager, to Europe and England to continue his education. John wanted to be a college professor, and he spent his years abroad specializing in German literature and becoming proficient in that language.[7] He made several "tours" of the Continent with the Reverend Eaton from Trinity Episcopal Church and finally returned home to Texas after contracting a severe case of pneumonia at his English school.

Rebecca and the children may have returned to Galveston from Houston for short or even extended periods during the war, but the whereabouts of James Brown has always puzzled *Ashton Villa* curators. Did he stay on the island, close to his businesses? If so, he must have led a very quiet life, for no contemporary accounts of Galveston's war years mention him.

And was there any business to hold him in the city? Many stores closed during the last stages of the conflict, and The Strand was virtually deserted. A famous illustration of the street from *Harper's Weekly*, made early in 1866, shows grass and weeds growing amongst the cobblestones.

Though he had opposed secession, James held two important positions in Confederate Texas: one as president of the Galveston, Houston & Henderson Railway, which exempted him from active military service, and two as a purchasing agent, negotiating the sale of Texas cotton through Mexican intermediaries for arms, ammunition, and medical supplies.[8] To aid the troops stationed in Galveston, Brown ordered the GH&H to extend tracks outward to service the new military posts established along the beachfront and east tip of the island. For these services, Confederate General John B. Magruder bestowed on James Brown the honorary title of Colonel.

And the Brown family continued to grow. Charles Rhodes was born early in 1862 and named for Rebecca's stepfather.

## ASHTON VILLA MYTHS

*Ashton Villa* took its place for the first time in Galveston mythology because of the war. Early in June 1865, Texas finally surrendered to the United States. A few weeks later, on June 19, General Gordon Granger declared General Order Number Three, which freed all slaves, to be effective in the state. It has long been said that this event took place from the second floor balcony of *Ashton Villa*, and that General Magruder also surrendered to Granger in the front parlour.

However, more careful reading of the documents makes it clear Granger spoke from his headquarters in the Osterman Building on The Strand, and that the surrender took place on board a Union vessel in the harbor. It has been said that *Ashton*

*Villa* was used as a hospital and a prison during the War, but this too is untrue.

James Brown, a Northerner by birth who doubtlessly watched the economic destruction of his adopted home with despair, was the first from the city to take the "Ironclad Oath." So anxious was he to reinstate his citizenship that he missed the birth of his last child, Matilda Ella (named for her aunt), on September 26, 1865. At that time he was in New York City, writing U.S. Secretary of State William H. Seward to accept the pardon issued to him in August.

## BUILDING A NEW FORTUNE

Contemporary sources declare that Brown lost his fortune because so much of it was tied up in slaves who were now free. However, that is incorrect on two counts: Brown owned only a few slaves, and he did not lose everything. Galveston County tax records for 1863 list him with $11,000 cash in hand, not a small amount of money, particularly in the midst of a war. His taxable wealth did indeed decline from $31,600 to $21,600 by 1864, but this "was primarily in 'money on hand and at interest,'" as *Ashton Villa* continued to retain much of its prewar value of $18,000.[9] And the GH&H Railway he managed emerged from the war in good shape, with net profits of nearly three quarters of a million dollars. J. M. Brown had rescued the line from penury, paid off its indebtedness, and actually declared dividends.

He soon resigned the presidency to focus his attention back on his hardware business and on rebuilding Galveston. Since his longtime partner Stephen Kirkland had died in 1859, Brown joined with German native J. W. Lang to open Brown & Lang Hardware on The Strand, where they profited by the wild surge of immigration and building that characterized Galveston after the war. Brown & Lang became a family business after John Stoddart returned from Europe and recovered from his illness. He joined his father's firm as a clerk and worked his way up through the ranks, moving out of *Ashton Villa* to live on Avenue G in the "western suburbs." In 1870 John married twenty-one-year-old Helen de Lespine. Five years later, on Lang's retirement, John became a full partner and the company was renamed J. S. Brown Hardware.

By the time his oldest son married, James Moreau Brown was the third wealthiest man in Galveston and ranked number five in the entire state. Census information, which tends to be conservative, listed him in 1870 as owning $175,000 worth of real estate and $100,000 in personal property. This was at a time when Reconstruction politics had beggared much of the old planter aristocracy but, conversely, raised the fortunes of merchants and businessmen who catered to the rapidly growing population and their needs.

## THE SPENDING '70S

What this meant for the Brown family and *Ashton Villa* was the beginning of an era of even greater affluence and power as they entered the decade of the 1870s. Bettie was a teenager growing into full adulthood during this time, and she may have begun to exert her first influence on the house then, for there is no reason to believe that her famous precociousness and determination were not longstanding characteristics.

Between 1874 and 1877 James and Rebecca Brown remodeled *Ashton Villa*, buying new furniture in the Renaissance Revival and Eastlake styles and replacing the old window valances inside the house with the incised and gilded walnut ones that still remain. Outside, the roof brackets were stylishly painted in several colors. The Browns also enclosed the space that had previously existed between the main house and the kitchen building to create what they called a dining hall much like a modern family room, complete with a skylight, baronial chandeliers, stuffed leather furniture, and a massive walnut

Bettie Brown about 1868, when she was thirteen years old. Note the elaborate coiffure, topped by a comb, and the many pieces of jewelry she is wearing. (Courtesy *Ashton Villa*)

This studio portrait of Bettie was made in St. Louis when she was about eighteen. Notice the elaborate and costly lace on her dress and the ever-present fan, this one of feathers. (Courtesy *Ashton Villa*)

fireplace surround. To the east end they attached a conservatory, the height of Victorian fashion.

On the other side was a bay, something like an open closet, that was built into the room rather than out beyond the exterior walls; its back wall consisted of floor-to-ceiling windows. Here in this sunny spot, the white Angora cats Bettie adored sunned themselves in what the Browns laughingly referred to as the "cats' parlour."[10] On the south side of the family room, the old exterior stairs once used by the servants for access to the house were replaced with new ones that led to the bedrooms on the second floor and afforded the children a way down without trampling through the "public" rooms.

There are no photographs of the house interior made after the remodeling to show what Bettie's bedroom looked like during her teen years. Its present furnishing is based on photos from the 1890s, and the only item left from this earlier period that would have been there during Bettie's adolescence is a large, leather-bound Bible given to her by her father on Bettie's nineteenth birthday (1874).

## MISS BETTIE

What influence Bettie may have had on *Ashton Villa's* improvements is not known. But it is evident from photographs that she began to assert herself as a young lady of fashion during the decade following the Civil War.

After completing whatever schooling she had by 1870,[11] Bettie began her life as an upper-class Victorian lady. The earliest known photo of her is one made a year or two earlier with best friend Maggie Vedder, who lived nearby. (Bettie later served as godmother to Maggie's daughter.) The two plump-cheeked girls, about thirteen or fourteen years old, are dressed as elaborately as their adult counterparts: striped satin dresses with large bustles (but with a shorter hem length as befits their age), jewelry, and a studiedly nonchalant pose.

This and other photographs of the young Bettie show a solemn teenager with a square face, an unblinking and direct expression, and the long, pointed Stoddart nose she and sister Matilda both inherited from their mother. Her coiffure is elaborate, even in the 1868 portrait: a tall coronet of braids, often surmounted by a comb, long ringlets, and a "fringe," or bangs. As she grew older, the ringlets disappeared.

What didn't change was the sumptuous clothing and jewelry, the latest fashions in satin and velvet worn with intricate, heavy gold earrings, necklaces, and bracelets. In one view, for example, made in a Denver studio sometime between 1872 and 1875, Bettie sports a large, trefoil pendant approximately five inches long, consisting of a large medallion on top and two smaller ones hanging from it, each set with what appears to be a carved cameo. On her right wrist is a wide gold bracelet, intricately chased, and a second bracelet on her other arm.

A Chicago portrait done in 1876 shows her with a gold "dog-collar" bangled necklace, a pearl-covered haircomb similar to one of hers still in *Ashton Villa*, bracelets, a ring, earrings, and a second, breast-length necklace strung with metal coins.

In many of these early views can also be seen Bettie's favorite collectible: fans. Feather fans, velvet and lace ones, painted examples, and carved ivory filled her drawers and complemented every costume. *Ashton Villa* still owns one painted with scenes of a Chinese court, and another depicting Grecian nymphs standing by a temple, both on display in her bedroom. And as many as a dozen other examples remain cherished family treasures. The collecting of fans was a passion that stayed with her the rest of her life.

This portrait of Bettie was made in Denver, Colorado, by Perry & Bohm Photo Studio, which operated from 1872 to 1875. (Courtesy *Ashton Villa*)

The studio portraits make it evident that Bettie had already begun the unceasing round of travels that would continue until ill health slowed her down in her late fifties and early sixties . . . Denver, Chicago, St. Louis, New York. Speculation that some of these trips were made in pursuit of her art studies cannot be verified.[12]

## THE BUDDING ARTIST

For art came to be her passion, first showing itself in the 1870s.

Amateur painting was a genteel and acceptable hobby for a woman of Bettie's social strata: it was cultural (therefore, in a woman's realm), could be accomplished without getting too dirty, and signalled the presence of wealth that provided ample leisure time for such pursuits. For many years, anything beyond mere "dabbling"—painting flowers on china or small landscapes one might give to Papa or a friend—was considered out of bounds for a true lady.

But the late nineteenth century saw a flowering of women artists in this country. Charlotte Streifer Rubinstein writes of this period: "Art, along with teaching, writing, and nursing, was one of the few respectable occupations open to the ever-growing number of unmarried or impoverished genteel women who needed some means of supporting themselves. . . . In addition . . . a number of upper-class women seeking outlets for their energy went into art as amateurs or cultural volunteers and found themselves irresistibly swept up into professionalism."[13] Among the latter, Bettie would come to include herself.

Probably the earliest surviving example of her work is a naive but exuberant field of sunflowers executed on wood, which still hangs in *Ashton Villa*. Soon after she embarked on a series of large scale oils painted on corduroy, possibly used because it was a cheaper or more available alternative to the then fashionable velvet canvas or because it created the effect of a tapestry. Described as "primitive" and "absurd,"[14] the five paintings from this period which remain in the mansion today depict young women dressed in idealized late eighteenth century peasant costumes. Two carry flowers, one is improbably placed in a cemetery holding a basket of cherries, and a fourth sits in a swing. Their expressions and poses are static, their smiles fixed; the women themselves are the primary or only subject.

In the fifth work, a woman in an Empire-style dress stands in a lush garden beside a fountain. Here she is almost subordinated to the depiction of the garden itself, and the style seems more mature and confident. This painting, which has hung in the front hall of *Ashton Villa* since it was executed, may represent a transition in Bettie's ability.[15]

Did her parents encourage Bettie? Apparently. For not only did they provide her with materials and, presumably, studio space, but they proudly hung her finished paintings in the house. The earliest interior photographs of *Ashton Villa* make clear that Bettie's art decorated the walls of the first floor from at least the early 1890s, when the views were made.

## MARDI GRAS

Her growing commitment to her art did not preclude Bettie from taking an active part in Galveston society, however; and her first big public "splash" came in 1876.

As early as 1867, Galveston, with its close commercial ties to New Orleans, had begun to observe Mardi Gras. Within a few years, this grew to a city-wide celebration with decorated wagons, torch-lit night parades, and several krewes which sponsored the festivities. In 1876 a new krewe made its appearance. The Mid-Day Revelers were assigned the duty of receiving Mighty Momus, the King of Mardi Gras, when he "arrived" at the port of Galveston on a U.S. Navy steamship.

The Revelers' procession to the harbor was a study in Oriental splendor. Roman nobles marched with Persian, Carthaginian, and Egyptian warriors, all lavishly mounted and costumed. Even Hannibal, "the Great Conqueror," deigned to participate as did Queen Esther. But it was Queen Cleopatra, as portrayed by Miss Rebecca Ashton Brown, who was the pièce de résistance. The Queen sat on her throne, surrounded by Nubian slaves and dressed in white and red, reported the *Galveston Daily News.* Four fluted columns supported the canopy under which she reclined, "the whole tastily [*sic*] and richly mounted and arranged." The *News* reporter covering the parade marveled at the "extravagance of the outlay necessary to produce the startling effects, the accuracy with which the most minute detail of Oriental habit was reproduced . . . and the fidelity to the . . . originals. . . ."

But Queen Cleopatra's triumph was short-lived in the newspaper. Far down in the list of the many women who attended the closing ball at the Opera House that evening was plain "Miss B. Brown."[16]

Bettie chose to memorialize her brief reign in a studio portrait made in Chicago. She sits in a chair on a raised platform, which allows the extravagant train of her lace dress to drape gracefully, and faces the camera with a satisfied expression. In her lap is a presentation box, and above it she holds a gold-filled pin surmounted with a crown; from the bar beneath the crown hang the letters M, D, and R. The back of the pin, which today is on display in Galveston's Mardi Gras Museum, is inscribed to "Bettie Brown, First Queen" of the Mid-Day Revelers.

Family descendant J. M. Brown III recalls his father telling him that Bettie was also named Cotton Queen of Texas one year, but the author was unable to confirm it. If true, she would have reigned over Waco's festival as Galveston did not begin its own "Kotton Karnival" until late in the century.

Chicago's Imperial Portrait Studio shot this portrait of Bettie holding the pin she received as first queen of the krewe of the Mid-Day Revelers in Galveston's 1876 Mardi Gras. On her lap is the presentation box. (Courtesy of Rosenberg Library, Galveston, Texas)

## SOCIAL WHIRL

The Browns were at the center of Galveston society. Mrs. Brown's especial forte was the New Year's Day reception, a favorite component of the city's social calendar, when most of the large homes were open for callers.

S. B. Southwick, one of the earliest residents of Galveston, recalled the happy scene: "The centers of gaiety . . . were the beautiful residences of Gen. E. B. Nichols, who lived on Broadway where the palatial Sealy house now stands [next door to *Ashton Villa*], and the magnificent home of Mrs. J. M. Brown . . . where [guests] found everything as beautiful, lovely and entertaining as they could wish. Those who called there were expected to attend her magnificent Ball that night."[17]

Galvestonians were not the only ones impressed by *Ashton Villa*.

In March of 1880 the city was honored by a visit from former President of the United States Ulysses S. Grant, who, with his wife and a party of other officers such as Phil Sheridan, was returning from a tour of Mexico. James Brown, as befitted one of the business community's leading lights, was present at all functions Grant attended, even riding with him in his private carriage on several tours of the city. But the Browns' coup came the day of a public reception held at the charming Nicholas Clayton-designed Garten Verein, a dance and social pavilion. Though already late, Grant and his entourage stopped to visit the family and marvel at the luxurious *Ashton Villa*, the only private residence they saw during their four-day stay.[18] Bettie was no doubt present to receive these distinguished guests with her parents; and who can say but that she proudly pointed out her own paintings to the one-time resident of the White House?

## Notes: Chapter Two

1   Howard Barnstone, *The Galveston That Was*, page 55.

2   For an excellent discussion on the building of *Ashton Villa*, see Kenneth Hafertepe, *A History of Ashton Villa*.

3   "The ordinance giving A. F. James and his associates the privilege of introducing gas into this city, was passed December 3d, 1855." *Galveston City Directory*, 1859-1869. The company actually opened in 1856.

4   The 1860 Slave Schedule for Galveston County lists only four slaves for J. M. Brown: a woman aged 35, a girl of 15, a 33-year-old man, and a 6-month-old girl.

    Interestingly, Brown does not appear on the 1850 Schedule, though it is known he did own slaves at that time. However, the family also does not appear on the Population Schedule that year, leading to the conclusion that they were residing somewhere out of Galveston at that time, possibly in New York on an extended visit.

5   Hafertepe, page 19. Barnstone, pages 55-56. *Ashton Villa* is often said to have been the first brick residence built in Texas.

6   S. B. Southwick, *Galveston Old and New*, page 9.

7   William Manning Morgan, in his 1954 history of Trinity Church, states that John met sculptor Elizabet Ney at a court ball for the King of Bavaria, and that when she moved to Austin, their friendship continued. However, the staff of the Elizabet Ney Museum in Austin can find no reference to any of the Browns in Miss Ney's records.

8   J. M. Brown was not alone in his opposition to secession. Among the more prominent figures arguing against it was former president of the Republic, and later governor, Sam Houston, who lost that office because he refused to take the oath of allegiance to the Confederacy.

9　Original 1863 tax receipt in the Galveston-Texas History Center, Rosenberg Library.

Untitled and incomplete history of Galveston and *Ashton Villa* in the collection of *Ashton Villa*, page 35 fin.

Most of Brown's slaves refused to leave after they became free; it is said that J. M. Brown provided them homes until their deaths and then, a funeral. His obituary, in speaking of his generosity, states that the former Brown slaves "have made it a rule [since emancipation] to appear at the old home and cook Christmas dinner and enjoy a reunion with the family. . . ."

10　Bettie's cats have been variously described as white Persians and as white Angoras. Though the two breeds are considered quite distinct today, in Bettie's time the names were almost interchangeable. Both are longhaired cats with ancient pedigrees that trace back to Persia and to the Sea of Ankara in Turkey.

11　In Galveston, after the war, Bettie likely attended a private dame school or the academy operated by the Ursuline order of nuns on the island.

12　The Art Institute of Chicago, for example, where Bettie is said to have studied, has no record of her from the time of the school's establishment in 1879 to 1892.

13　*American Women Artists from Early Indian Times to the Present*, pages 91-92.

14　Barnstone, *op. cit.*, page 56.

15　None of the corduroy paintings are dated; indeed, only a few of Bettie's works are, which makes placing them in a chronology difficult.

16　*Galveston Daily News*, March 1, 1876, page 1.

The *News* coverage does not name the persons acting the roles of the various characters in the parade. Nor do the records of the Galveston-Texas History Center at the Rosenberg Library provide names. The author's assumption that Bettie portrayed Cleopatra rather than Esther is based on the fact that her pin is inscribed to her as the "First Queen" of the krewe, and that Cleopatra's float was the showpiece of the parade, as would befit the "main" queen.

17    Southwick, *op. cit.*, page 8.

18    For accounts of Grant's visit, *see Galveston Daily News*, March 23-26, 1880.

# CHAPTER THREE

# Around the World . . .

Bettie's travels during the 1870s were domestic, but in 1881 she followed her brothers Charles and Moreau overseas to Europe for the first time.

## THE BROWN BOYS

John Stoddart had set the trend for the Brown offspring to study abroad with his Civil War sojourn in England and Germany. But by 1880 he was firmly fixed in Galveston, having succeeded John Lang as partner upon his retirement in 1875. Having now renamed the business J. S. Brown & Company, John's father turned the operations over to him while he concentrated on other endeavors. The Galveston community considered John Stoddart "a young man brimming over with enterprise and energy," whose prospects were "brilliant."[1] The first of John and Helen's three daughters, another Rebecca Ashton Brown (known as Reba, to distinguish her from her aunt Bettie and her grandmother), was born about the time the family moved into *Live Oak Terrace*, a Greek Revival house just two blocks up Broadway from *Ashton Villa*. John emulated his father in using only the best material for construction: lumber from South America and ornamentation such as the stone lions at the entrance imported from Europe.

The second Brown son, Moreau, after briefly clerking in his father's hardware store, entered medical school in Kentucky and graduated in 1876. He married Alice Jane Daugherty and brought her home to Galveston, where he opened a practice. Moreau was appointed the city's quarantine officer in 1879 and implemented policies to reduce the yellow fever problem.

Charles Rhodes would prove to be the adventuresome son, taking after his father. He started school in Galveston, then went on to Racine College in Wisconsin in preparation for joining the Episcopalian ministry, a goal he eventually put aside.[2] Like his brother Moreau, who had studied briefly in Philadelphia, Charles returned to their mother's birthplace to apprentice as a watchmaker. By the early 1880s, not yet married, he was ready to venture abroad.

## TO EUROPE

Bettie too was anxious for the adventure, and with Charles, Moreau, his wife Alice Jane, and their son James Moreau II (born 1877), she embarked for two years in Europe sometime in 1881. Once there, the three siblings scattered to their various studies, rejoining at least once to vacation together. Charles studied stone engraving and cameo cutting, and Moreau divided his time between Germany and Austria, where he began his concentration in diseases of the nose and throat.[3]

Bettie also selected Munich and Vienna as her two home bases. Since she had already been "out" for years, it's not likely that her parents considered this trip the finishing touch to her education enjoyed by so many young women of her class. More probable is that the Browns were encouraging Bettie in her art.

Where, and under whom, to study, however, caused her problems.

Europe was the mecca for a woman artist—or, indeed, any other—in Bettie's day. But even there, many state-run academies did not accept women either as pupils or teachers, and those that did usually prohibited them from life drawing—sketching a nude model—which was "training considered essential to an artist's development."[4] Paris' Ecole des Beaux-Arts, for example, admitted women students in 1896 only after they literally stormed the building. And in Germany, most female artists studied at "Damenakademies" such as the Verein School for Women in Berlin (established 1868).

The alternative was private tutoring.

Descendants state that Bettie took lessons from the court painter of Austria-Hungary's Emperor Franz Joseph (1830-1916), but records are very scarce and do not yet confirm that. However, the fact that she did have social contact with the Austrian royal family over the years tends to verify this story.

The other possibility must be gleaned from Bettie's work itself. The paintings she completed during this period suggest that she changed techniques from a more stilted style to a new one called fast brush painting. Developed in Munich by American artists William Merritt Chase (who later numbered Georgia O'Keefe among his pupils) and Frank Duveneck, the fast brush technique was quicker, bolder, "without too much overworking." Detailed pencil sketches were discarded for charcoal drawings. The subject matter changed, too, romanticized and picturesque peasants and landscapes replacing classical and mythological themes.

Whether Bettie studied directly under Chase or Duveneck, or under another artist influenced by them, is not known. But the change in her style, and the fact of her part-time residence in Munich during those artists' heyday, points to her deliberate choice of the fast brush technique. She also changed her palette, the pastels of her early corduroys giving way to rich jewel tones and, in some cases, sombre shadings.

## FINISHED WORKS

Still in *Ashton Villa* today are at least six or seven works of art known or thought to have been done by Bettie while in Europe. "Still Life of Peacock and Wine Glass" is an oil on canvas, signed and dated by her "1882 Wien" (*i.e.*, Vienna). "Still Life of Mandolin and Feather Fan" has no assignation, but donor information states that it hung in her sister Matilda's house after she married in 1884; that, along with its similarity to the previous work, would indicate it, too, was done in Europe.[5]

The third oil painting has long posed a dilemma for *Ashton Villa* curators. Is "Lady in Evening Dress" (Munich, 1883) a self-portrait, or does it represent Matilda? The two women looked almost identical in profile, as is the woman in this work. It was clearly painted in Munich, for the gilt frame still bears the label of the framer there, which leads most to believe that it is Bettie. But the woman's hair is red—Bettie was a blonde, further clouding the identification.

The remaining works are charcoal sketches, including one of a woman wearing a Dutch sunbonnet which was found beneath "Lady in Evening Dress" when it was cleaned in 1988. The bold, broad lines here are the same as in "The Shepherd" and "The Shepherdess," separate works depicting two young people wearing European peasant costumes and signed by Bettie in 1882. These three, along with "Lady in Evening Dress," most clearly demonstrate Bettie's flirtation with fast brush drawing and demonstrate a greatly matured ability from the earlier corduroy paintings.

A seventh work, "Lady in a Black Mantilla," was likely done in Europe, too, and probably represents a favorite technique of art students: copying the works of another painter. This portrait of a harsh-featured older woman, possibly from the Mediterranean region, is easily the darkest of Bettie's surviving works.[6]

Her art was never professional, in the sense that she sold any pieces. All of Bettie's known work either remains in *Ashton Villa* where it has hung for a hundred years, or was given to family and friends. Moreover, she does not seem to have joined any major art organizations.[7] Bettie's painting was for her amusement only. It satisfied her creative bent, but was it also an outlet for energies that society would not let her channel any other way? Later records and her own activities indicate that Bettie was extremely organized, efficient, and diplomatic in handling others, talents she inherited from her father. She would have made an excellent administrator, but Victorian society prohibited that. Did she push the boundaries of what was acceptable—even in an area as genteel as art—out of frustration? Only Bettie knew, and she left no surviving record of her feelings.

## TO THE MEDITERRANEAN

Life in Europe was not all work for the Brown siblings.

Unfortunately, only one photograph has survived from their vacations together, traveling about the continent and the Mediterranean. In 1882 the family journeyed south to Italy and, among other sites, visited Pompeii, buried in a volcanic eruption in A.D. 79. A photo shows the five, with a guide, on the steps of the Temple of Isis. Charles' diary of their trip was later given away and then destroyed, and his photo album was lost in the 1900 Storm; so researchers can piece together virtually nothing of their itinerary.

There was plenty of amusement to enjoy while living in their temporary European homes of Munich and Vienna: the marriage of Austria's Crown Prince Rudolph to Princess Stephanie in 1881; the celebration of the 600th anniversary of Austria and the Hapsburg dynasty (1882); art museums, parks, coffeehouses. The ongoing construction of Vienna's Ringstrasse, the broad boulevard begun by Franz Joseph in

1857 which helped preserve Vienna's green space as the population of the city doubled. The gardens of Schonbrunn Palace and the art treasures housed in the Liechenstein family palace.

Not that Europe was all fun. In 1882, while Bettie was there, Vienna was the scene of some of the worst street fights in decades, as rich and poor clashed violently.

Bettie doubtlessly began her famous collection of travel artifacts while in Europe. She loved to shop—as one friend would later put it, "she had it bad"—and had the wealth to indulge herself. Over the next decades, she would fill *Ashton Villa* with the fruits of those binges: textiles, jewelry, folk art, crystal, silver and more were carefully shipped back to Galveston and placed about the mansion to entertain family and visitors. By the early 1890s she had collected so many that she persuaded her father to renovate a small room, or closet, located at the north end of the reception room and also opening into the family dining hall, where she displayed her treasures, which included more than one hundred silver baskets ranging in size from one inch to three feet tall.[8]

Nor did she forget the family back in Galveston during this European interlude. Matilda Brown's surviving diary from the first half of 1883 contains references to fifteen letters written her by Bettie; unfortunately, they have not survived, and Matilda did not describe the contents in her diary.

Bettie and her companions sit on the steps of the Temple of Isis on their 1882 visit to Pompeii, Italy. Left to right: James Moreau Brown II; his father, Dr. Moreau Brown (Bettie's brother); Moreau's wife, Jane; Bettie's brother Charles Rhodes Brown; Bettie; and an Italian guide. (Courtesy *Ashton Villa*)

## Notes: Chapter Three

1 Charles W. Hayes, *Galveston: History of the Island and City*, page 973.

2 Phone interview with Mrs. T. J. Stanly, great-granddaughter of Charles Rhodes Brown.

3 Vienna's medical schools were considered among the best in the world at this time and attracted students from everywhere, especially America, where medical studies were still in their infancy. To attend or graduate from Vienna conferred great prestige.

4 Rubinstein, *op. cit.*, pages 92-93.

5 Bettie apparently painted these from arranged settings. A photo of her in the Gold Room of *Ashton Villa* (circa 1892) shows the mandolin and a brass Mideastern, hookah-type device that appears in one of the paintings, both of which are sitting on the piano.

Howard Barnstone, in his book *The Galveston That Was* (1966), was not a fan of Bettie's artistic abilities. "She had studied abroad for many years," he wrote, "and, since she had traveled throughout the Old World, she brought back relics and costumes from every part, which she sometimes unhappily conveyed to canvas." page 56.

6 The possibility of finding previously unknown works by Bettie in other collections is exciting for *Ashton Villa* curators and for Bettie researchers. But because she didn't always sign her paintings, attributing them with any certainty can be chancy.

Recently discovered in the Bay Area Museum at Seabrook, Texas is a large, almost full-size, corduroy painting in a style very much like Bettie's. It depicts a woman in Grecian dress standing in a rural landscape and holding a long garland of greens and flowers. Is it Bettie's? That's hard to say. The technique and subject matter certainly look like her; the blades of grass in the foreground, for example, appear identical in execution to those in "Lady by a Fountain" which hangs in the hallway at *Ashton Villa.* But there is no signature.

Another mystery revolves around a painting in one of Galveston's historic houses, the *Mistrol-Paul House,* built in 1896 by East Texas dry goods scion Felix Mistrol and purchased shortly after the 1900 Storm by the Paul family, friends of the Browns. Still hanging on the stairway landing is a large corduroy that is the only survivor of a triptych, seen in an early photograph of the house. This large central painting depicts a sea nymph rising from the water, a cherub band whirling about her head and playing their instruments. (Cherubs, of course, were one of Bettie's favorite subjects for a time.) The two smaller works, known only from the photo, show the same nymph either rising higher from the water or descending. The current owners of the house believe they may have a work by Miss Bettie, who was a good friend of the Pauls; additional support for their claim comes from the fact that one of the Pauls married a Vedder, the same family as Bettie's longtime friend Maggie Vedder. But without a signature, they cannot verify it.

7    The author queried numerous art schools and organizations still in existence that date from Bettie's day but was unable to find any record of her.

8    In addition to silver, Bettie also had white wicker baskets lined with turquoise velvet for her cats.

.    .    .    .

CHAPTER FOUR

# A Lady of Fashion

While Bettie was passing through her mid-twenties in Europe, her younger sister Matilda stayed in Galveston, where she enjoyed an adolescence probably very similar to Bettie's after the Civil War.

## THE DIARY

Matilda, or Tillie as the family called her, kept a diary, but only a few months' entries (February-June, 1883) have survived. The seventeen-year-old Matilda went to the theater, visited on the new-fangled telephone, attended church, and practiced at her piano. She, her girlfriends, and their beaus danced at receptions in the Artillery Hall, took horseback rides, and regularly "went down the island," riding in wagons along the beach to Galveston's West End. Matilda occasionally visited Dickinson (a favorite train excursion for Galvestonians), Houston, and the health spa at Sour Lake near Beaumont. On Wednesday afternoons the *Ashton Villa* ladies were "At Home" to receive guests and have tea, a highly ritualized activity for women of the Browns' social stature. It was a

Portrait of Bettie's sister, Matilda Ella Brown, known as Tillie to her family. Justus Zahn Studio fo Galveston made this study about the time of Matilda's 1884 wedding to Thomas H. Sweeney. (Courtesy of Rosenberg Library, Galveston, Texas)

genteel and leisurely life that Matilda does not seem to have rebelled against.[1]

By the time Bettie and her brothers returned from Europe, Matilda had met Thomas H. Sweeney, born in Boston and an employee of the J. Moller & Co. shipping firm of Galveston. Her diary reveals the ups and downs of their early courtship but ends just before Sweeney himself left for Europe on vacation.[2] Despite a somewhat rocky start, and the fact that Sweeney was nearly twice her age, Matilda eventually agreed to marry him sometime in late 1883.

The ceremony took place at Trinity Episcopal Church the evening of May 7, 1884, the chapel lavishly decorated with flowers and ferns and with a standing-room-only crowd—both inside and outside the church—to see the spectacle. The *Galveston Daily News* enthused that Matilda's event ranked "in supremacy in points of fashionable attendance and accompanying eclat" far ahead of the forty other weddings held in the city that spring.

Mrs. Brown wore black velvet and satin with diamonds, while Matilda was a traditional bride in heavy white satin, point lace, and orange blossoms, with diamond earrings given her by Thomas. Half of her six attendants were dressed in pink, the others in blue.

But Bettie, who with brother Charles followed Matilda's attendants in the processional, pleased the crowd by wearing a petticoat of cream white silk with an overdress of Mechlin and Irish point lace, "the corsage cut decolette"—that is, low cut—and "a necklace of African beetles," probably Egyptian scarabs purchased in the Mediterranean.

*Ashton Villa* was a "scene of brilliance" for the reception, with many other family members present: Sarah Stoddart Rhodes (Mrs. Brown's mother); John Stoddart and Helen Brown; Matilda Garlick (Mrs. Brown's sister) and her daughter, who was an attendant; and Mr. and Mrs. C. C. Sweeney

(Thomas' brother and his wife), whose daughter Jenny was also a bridesmaid. In addition, many representatives of Galveston's "upper crust" crowded into *Ashton Villa* for the festivities.

Matilda and Thomas left afterward for a honeymoon of "several months travelling through the great West and Northwest."[3] When they returned, it was to live only a few blocks from the Browns on Avenue L, in a frame house built by James Brown and presented to his daughter as a wedding gift.[4]

Such a fairy tale start to a marriage should have augured well for its success, but that was not to be the case with the Sweeneys. And the eventual disintegration of Matilda's relationship with her husband had a profound impact on Bettie.

## BETTIE'S BEAUS

Bettie continued her butterfly existence through the 1880s, traveling, flirting, and partying. In St. Louis she had two wonderful portraits made of herself.

In one, from F. W. Guerin Studio, she reclines at her leisure in a chair, legs crossed shockingly at the knees, a slight smile on her face, and holding one of her favorite feather fans over her shoulder in a most nonchalant manner. She wears a sleeveless velvet dress with pearls in her hair. It is decidedly *not* a typical pose of an upper-class Victorian lady.

The second—also made by Guerin, but a few years later, in 1884 or 1885—is equally marvelous, for it depicts Bettie with two of her male admirers. Again, she leans back in a chair, but this time her gloved hands are folded demurely in her lap, and her legs are crossed unusually, but not outrageously so, at the ankles. The gentlemen, with their elegant waxed mustachios and macassared hair, lean toward her almost leeringly, while Bettie gives them a look as if to say, "Keep your distance, boys." Miss Rebecca Ashton Brown was not only pretty and flirtatious but a considerable heiress—a potent combination.

Bettie struck this divine pose in the St. Louis studio of F.W. Guerin sometime in the late 1870s. Guerin (1846-1903) was known for his "artistic" and nontraditional approach to portraiture. (Courtesy *Ashton Villa*)

Little is known about her admirers except that they were reported to be numerous: her niece Alice Sweeney Jumonville always asserted that Bettie's "suitors were many, here and abroad." A silver trophy bowl in the dining room of *Ashton Villa* is said to have been given her by Nichols Stuart; another beau is said to have drunk champagne from one of her gilded slippers. And a member of the Levy family who recently visited *Ashton Villa* swears that its tradition holds Bettie was "kept" by one of the original Levy brothers, who paid for her New York hotels and other luxuries.[5] This story, however, is completely unsubstantiated and is an example of the kinds of rumors that often surrounded an unmarried woman of Bettie's day.

One of the most persistent stories about Bettie alleges that she became pregnant by the family's coachman, who was a Negro, and that was the reason for her long sojourn in Europe. An interesting tale, particularly since census records show the postwar coachmen at *Ashton Villa* to have been young, white Europeans.[6] And the dramatic improvement in Bettie's artistic ability after her trip argues that she spent most of her time there profitably in her studies, not engaged in the emotional and time consuming roller-coaster of giving birth and then finding a family to adopt the baby.

## STAYING SINGLE

The fact is that Bettie kept as quiet about her gentlemen friends as she did so many other aspects of her life. Did she remain single by choice? Or was hers the role often given to the older daughter in a Victorian home, that of caretaker for aged parents? Commonly held myth today declares that women of this era believed marriage was the only acceptable life choice, but that is incorrect. Particularly after the Civil War, a number of American women elected to remain single. They may have done so from the shortage of men or from a very real fear of childbirth and the high possibility of permanent complications or death that often accompanied it. A simple love of independence may have been the reason, or a desire to devote time to some social or philanthropic cause. There was also an economic factor, since married women legally surrendered their property and its management to their husbands, a coercion distasteful to those perfectly capable of overseeing their own holdings. Often these single women were of wealth and standing and could afford the luxury of such a lifestyle.

In Bettie's case, the reason for her spinsterhood is not clear. Certainly she enjoyed an independent life of travel and work that Matilda—for whatever reason—did not. Bettie was also very close to her father. James Brown's 1895 obituary states, "His contributions to charity, it is said, are known only to his youngest [sic] daughter, Miss Bettie, who shared his confidence to a degree that marked the most tender companionship between father and daughter." Perhaps that very closeness led her to embrace the eventual position of caregiver, and, in return, her father encouraged her art and her liberty. Certainly he must have seen in her the same drive and "thirst for freedom" that he also possessed.[7] His own unconventional youth likely made him impatient of the strict mores that governed most women in his day. Since money, in his opinion, was not to be hoarded but used to "surround his family with comforts and advantages" and "to make those around and about him happy," Brown allowed his daughter all the funds she required for her various ventures.[8]

In *Ashton Villa*, that spirit was expressed in her suite of rooms. After Matilda married and moved to her own home, Bettie took over the northwest bedroom on the second floor that had belonged to her and remodeled it for a study. These rooms were so beautifully appointed that they were well known in Galveston. When Mrs. Brown's widowed niece, Sallie May Garlick Ferrier, returned to spend the summer of 1885 at *Ashton Villa*, the *Opera Glass* noted that she was "comfortably located, having by right of connection so harmoniously grafted herself . . . into the personel [*sic*] of the family as to be granted the use of Miss Bettie Brown's elegant and luxurious apartments."[9] Bettie, to judge from that report, had long since left the city for the summer.

## SUMMERING IN WAUKESHA

Galveston's social season ended with Lent and Easter, and the city's extremely hot and humid summers were added inducements for the elite to travel to cooler climes where "the season" was just beginning. One of Bettie's favorite destinations was the resort town of Waukesha, Wisconsin, located near Milwaukee and known as the Saratoga of the West.

She made her first trip there about 1879 and always stayed at the Fountain Springs Hotel (rebuilt 1878-1879 after a fire), a favorite summering spot of Chicago politicians. So constant was she in traveling there about mid-June that staff and townspeople came to consider Bettie's arrival the real opening of the season.

Miss Brown swirled into the hotel with a "retinue of negro servants" to see to her comfort as well as her own carriage, liverymen, coachman and horses, and sixteen trunks "filled with such finery as local residents never before beheld on one woman." Inside were exquisite examples of couture such as her black velvet gown with fall leaves embossed in solid gold on the court train and an ostrich fan studded with pearls. Visitors remembered for years the grand ball that opened the 1893 season: Bettie wore an emerald green brocaded satin dress with train and velvet balloon sleeves, diamond earrings, and "a necklace of amethysts in Tuscan gold." She always led the grand march at the opening ball, partnered with such well-known men as Colonel Richard Dunbar, owner of the Bethesda Springs resort. Despite her opulence, the belle from Texas was well liked in Waukesha, for she was never a "snob."[10]

Never to be forgotten was the day Bettie's horses ran away with her and her friends.

Bettie had invited Carrie Nickell and Bessie Sanford for a drive, and the girls were delighted to find her distinguished-looking coachman on the box. But "our hearts went down and we had our own misgivings," remembered Miss Nickell, when Bettie appeared and dismissed him, taking the reins herself. The horses were "fractious" and the girls "very timid . . . But as we had seen Bettie drive many times alone, we tried to feel that she could handle them just as skillfully now as she had at other times."

Something frightened the team, however, and they burst down the street, "busses and people dodging in our path to clear the way for us." Bettie remained calm and pulled at the horses' reins. When it became clear they were too much for her, she adjured her passengers to help her. "Pull, girls, pull!" The three finally got the team under control, and one of Bettie's liverymen, seeing them pass, helped bring the horses to a halt. "I shall never forget that ride," Miss Nickell assured a newspaper reporter.[11]

Bettie was also well known in Waukesha as an artist, leading to the conclusion that she did some painting there, though no remaining examples are known. Friends and "art critics" urged her to show her work in "well-known galleries," but she always refused.

## THE ADIRONDACKS . . .

After 1890 Bettie also spent some summers in the Adirondack Mountains of New York at a resort called Childwold Park. That mountainous region had recently become popular and, in 1889, Addison Child of Boston built a five-story hotel, individual cottages, bowling alley, casino, outbuildings, and trails along the shores of Lake Massawepie and the Raquette

River to cater to the merchant aristocracy of the Northeast. At 1,535 feet above sea level, it must have seemed like heaven to Galveston-bred Bettie.

One photograph survives of Bettie at Childwold Park, and it depicts her in a setting few would imagine for her—a tent. The huge canvas structures stood on raised wooden floors and, in the photo, Bettie peeps mischievously around the front upright of her tent on "Ghost Row."[12] According to a circa 1900 brochure on Hotel Childwold, tents such as this one could be rented by guests wishing to camp out along the banks of the lake.

There is one peculiar omission from these trips that is not at first apparent. The Adirondack Mountains have been the subject of countless paintings; Winslow Homer, for example, executed a number of works. But there is no similar work that can be attributed to Bettie. Did she not paint here? Perhaps she was dissatisfied with the results and destroyed them. All of her surviving pieces are either still lifes or portraits, and the lack of landscapes leads the researcher to conclude that they simply were not within the scope of her skills or interests.

## . . . AND THE CITY

Summers were spent in cool locations such as these, but for several months every fall and winter, Bettie took up residence in New York City. Access to New York in her day was easy: one simply boarded a steamer of the Mallory Line in Galveston and arrived on the East Coast a leisurely week later.

Descendants claim she maintained an apartment at the Waldorf-Astoria, but Victorian records of that hotel are scarce and contain no reference to her. The only hotels where she is known to have stayed were the Imperial (in 1897, on a trip with Matilda, Mrs. Brown, Mrs. John Sealy, and her daughter, Mrs. Smith) and the Empire. The latter was built about 1900 at

This charming and unusually candid view of Bettie was made at Childwold Park in the Adirondack Mountains of New York about 1895. The back is labeled "Fatty No. 1 - Ghost Row." (Courtesy *Ashton Villa*)

Broadway and 63rd Street and announced itself as "dedicated to those Sensible American People Who Seek Comfort Without Waste and Elegance Without Ostentation."[13]

In the city, Bettie shopped, toured the museums, had her portraits made at several photography studios she patronized, visited friends and family, and regularly embarked for Europe. She may also have studied art at a studio there.

And she had male admirers in New York.

In *The Browns of Ashton Villa*, Suzanne Morris quotes a poetic "Welcome to Miss Rebecca Brown," written by Larry Chittenden upon her arrival for the winter of 1902. Though he concentrates on Bettie's efforts to help Galveston after the devastating 1900 Storm, Chittenden does not neglect to mention that "this Texas Princess" was also charming, gay, and lovely.

Bettie was forty-seven years old at the time.

## MISS BETTIE REMODELS

By 1890 Galveston was truly the "Queen City of the Gulf" with a population of 29,000 and its now-grand residential boulevard, Broadway, increasingly lined with palatial homes. Walter Gresham had built his $250,000 mansion (today the *Bishop's Palace*), Narcissa Willis had erected the stone and brick structure later owned by W. L. Moody Jr., and, next door to *Ashton Villa*, George and Magnolia Willis Sealy had hired famed New York architect Stanford White to create a Chateauesque fantasy, *The Open Gates*.

Bettie looked about her and frowned.

*Ashton Villa* may have been the most elaborate and up-to-date house in Galveston, if not in Texas, when it was built; but now it was thirty years old and, in her opinion, showing its age. Familiar with the great palaces of the world, well aware that the latest vogue was for French Rococo Revival—and incensed that Magnolia Sealy was stealing her limelight—Bettie talked her parents into a second remodeling.

First to be done was the large west parlour or reception room which became, in blatant imitation of the Sealys, "the Gold Room." The original French style walnut furniture was painted white and gold and given new tapestry-like upholstery. Gilt cornices replaced the 1870s walnut ones, an Aubusson rug covered the floor, and the fireplace mantel also received a coat of the white and gold paint.

Following the current craze to cover every square inch of wallspace with decoration, Bettie filled the Gold Room with paintings, many of them her own work. She had recently completed a new series of corduroy paintings—much improved technically over her earlier work—built around both classical themes and the cupids and cherubs popularized by French artist William Bouguereau.

By the south door leading into the hall she hung a large piece depicting a cherub surrounded by garlands of flowers; this work of hers no longer exists and is known only through a

Members of the Brown family gathered in the Gold Room for a five-generation portrait to commemorate the birth of Reba Brown McClanahan's son, John, on November 28, 1891. Left to right: the baby's grandmother Helen de Lespine Brown (Mrs. John Stoddart Brown holding the baby), James Moreau and Rebecca Stoddart Brown (the baby's great-grandparents), Sarah Stoddart Rhodes (Mrs. Brown's mother) and her second husband Charles Rhodes. (Courtesy of Rosenberg Library, Galveston, Texas)

photograph of the Gold Room. By the opposite door, she placed "Grecian Girl with Urn," and next to it was her rendition of Bouguereau's "First Kiss."[14] This latter work depicted nude cherubs, or "putti," and was originally framed with lace curtains that could be closed to avoid offending the too sensitive. Later Bettie moved it to an adjacent wall and took down the curtains. She also did a second version which featured only the heads and shoulders of the models; it hung on the west wall of the Gold Room.[15] What's interesting about Bettie's "First Kiss" is that it is not a faithful copy of Bouguereau's work, but her own interpretation. And in it, she returned to the pastel colors of her first corduroys, executed several decades earlier.

A very different work, "Lady in a Black Mantilla," was either copied from another artist's work or was executed while Bettie, Charles, and Moreau vacationed in Europe in the early 1880s. It is very dark in tone and features a harsh-faced woman, perhaps of Mediterranean origin, wearing a black cap tied under her chin and a black lace mantilla.

Bettie filled the remaining spaces with the bric-a-brac so beloved by the Victorians: gilt china cabinets, crystal lustres, examples of her basket collection, marble pedestals, and small pieces of sculpture.

Other paintings of Bettie's were hung in the ladies' parlour and dining room across the hall, the most striking example being "Lady in Red." It is an oil painting depicting a young woman in vaguely Renaissance dress, red with red and white slashed sleeves, lace collar, and feathered hat. In the dining room is another oil, "Lady in Peasant Costume," a profile study of a woman wearing a red and green scarf turban. A third still life may also date from this period, a softly faded view of a pair of red satin shoes with an ivory stick fan and string of pearls.

The dining room was filled with china, crystal, and silver, the latter of which Bettie collected extensively. There were massive handled trays, heavy with scrollwork and engraved

In the newly remodeled Gold Room of *Ashton Villa* (circa 1892), Bettie arranges flowers in one of her many silver baskets. To the left, behind the piano, is the entrance to the room where she displayed her travel items. To the right hang Bettie's rendition of Bouguereau's "First Kiss" and "Grecian Girl with Urn." On the piano are several items which appeared in other paintings of hers. (Courtesy of Rosenberg Library, Galveston, Texas)

"RAB." Presentation bowls and compotes—many of them also engraved—and more of her treasured silver baskets stood cheek-by-jowl in the china cabinets and on the shelves lined with her favorite turquoise velvet in the "butler's pantry." In accordance with the strict and elaborate Victorian rituals surrounding dining, Bettie laid the table with every manner of silver serving piece: tongs only used for picking up asparagus, ice cream forks and knives, a fruit knife for peeling oranges, and forks just for eating the oysters plucked from Galveston's waters . . . all in addition to the regular tableware. She lavishly

Bettie's bedroom after the circa 1890 remodeling. (Courtesy of Rosenberg Library, Galveston, Texas)

decorated the table with flowers and greens from her mother's gardens, presented in their own silver containers.

Upstairs in her private suite of rooms, she added a white and gold fireplace mantel and surround which is topped with a mirror that was tilted forward—according to family lore—so that Bettie might see herself entering the room. But she also placed a carved, mahogany double bed against the north wall (adjoining the sitting room); this effectively blocked the door

Another view of Bettie's bedroom after the circa 1890 remodeling. (Courtesy of Rosenberg Library, Galveston, Texas)

into that room and belies the family story of the mirror. Filmy lace curtains hung across and alongside the headboard to break up the bed's massive lines.

A matching dresser sat opposite the fireplace; among the ornaments on its surface was a painter's palette that had been converted to a clock. Bettie's dresser set, which is still in her room, featured a sea motif. Above were compartments for facepowder and hairpins, and a bud vase for a fresh flower on the top, the whole decorated with cherubs and shells. A brass basket held two turquoise glass bottles with lids in the form of coral branches. Unfortunately, the wonderful brass dragonfly that once adorned the dresser set has been stolen.

As in the Gold Room, the bedroom was cluttered with paintings, photographs, corner "bric-a-brac" shelves, clocks, and Turkish-style area rugs atop the floral carpet. It was an intensely feminine and unmistakably Victorian room. In the adjoining office or sitting room, she added another new mantelpiece, this one in an asymmetrical "Oriental" design. No photo has survived of this room, so little is known of how she completed its furnishings.

Bettie supervised all these changes to the house, as well as those made in other rooms. Family members recall that she was not above climbing a ladder herself to show erring workmen exactly what she wanted done.

## THE WORLD'S FAIR

One of Bettie's first philanthropic endeavors, aside from the work she did with her father, was to raise money for the Texas Building at the 1893 Columbian World Exposition in Chicago. The state legislature had refused to vote funds for the structure, claiming Texas' constitution prohibited such an expenditure. So two volunteer organizations took up the task, the Gentlemen's World's Fair Association of Texas and the Texas Women's World's Fair Association.

Upon the women fell the bulk of the work to raise the money needed. The Board of Lady Managers was headed by Austin artist Bernadette Tobin, who rallied everyone from schoolchildren to the state lumbermen's association to pitch in. Mrs. Tobin's main focus, however, was Texas women; and she asserted that their "chief object . . . this winter should be to assist in raising the money necessary for the erection of the

Texas Building at Chicago." Texans responded with fervor, and the ladies turned in more than $30,000 to build and furnish the structure.[16]

Bettie served on the Galveston committee and also toured the Fair as the city's representative. Although there was a separate Women's Building in which America's female artists were encouraged to display their work, Bettie apparently did not exhibit any of her own pieces in either building.

Of course, she was also in Chicago from time to time over the years, visiting brother Moreau and his family; and several formal portraits of her made in studios there have survived.[17]

Bettie must have felt at home with the many forthright and active ladies involved in the Chicago Fair. In her guide to the Women's Building, author Maude Elliott Howe expressed the changing status and role of women in 1893: "The World's Columbian Exposition has afforded woman an unprecedented opportunity to present to the world a justification of her claim to be placed on complete equality with man . . . Twenty years ago to be called strong-minded was a reproach which brought the blood to the cheek of many a woman. To-day [sic] there are few of our sisters who do not prefer to be classed among strong-minded rather than among weak-minded women."[18]

## Notes: Chapter Four

1   Charles Brown's great-granddaughter, Mrs. T. J. Stanly, says that her mother remembers Matilda as "the motherly type" who enjoyed the management of the house and children.

2   On August 26, 1883, the *Opera Glass*, Galveston's society paper, quoted "as follows from a private letter from Mr. Thomas H. Sweeney: 'I have just returned from a trip through Russia, Denmark, France and Germany, and am here (Venice) enjoying the scenery and climate. I shall take a turn through Italy and another short trip through France, and will then feel like returning to Galveston and to work.'"

Thomas Sweeney's brother, C. C. (1838-1892), lived in Galveston, too, and was likewise involved in shipping. Born in Boston, C. C. moved to Galveston in 1856 and was a "prime mover" in organizing the Galveston & Liverpool Steamship Co., with vessels specially designed for the cotton trade. He also owned five sailing ships, one of them named for his younger brother Thomas. C.C. was Collector of the Port of Galveston 1885-1889, a strong Texas Democrat, and the owner of one of the city's largest private libraries. The Miss Sweeney who served as an attendant in Matilda and Thomas' wedding was likely his daughter Jennie (later Mrs. J. D. Buckley). (From *History of Texas, Together With a Biographical History of the Cities of Houston and Galveston*.)

3   Description of the wedding from *Galveston Daily News*, May 8, 1884.

4   The Sweeney-Royston House, which still stands at 2402 Avenue L, was long said to have been designed by premier Galveston architect Nicholas Clayton, but there is no documentary evidence to support this. Clayton did design the J. S. Brown Hardware Company building at

2111, The Strand, now the home of "Colonel Bubbie's" army surplus.

5    Letter to the author from Beth Weidler, January 15, 1996. Levy Bros. Department Store was a longtime fixture in the Galveston business community.

6    In 1880 the *Ashton Villa* coachman was William Clawsen, age 29, born in Switzerland. In 1890 Herman Testica (?), also 29, a native of Germany served.

7    Suzanne Morris, *The Browns of Ashton Villa*, np.

8    Obituary of James M. Brown.
     By the mid-1880s, his wealth and position in Galveston had grown even greater. J. M. Brown was a founder and president of First National Bank (the first national bank in Texas) and served a term as president of the Texas Bankers Association; was a founder, director, and officer of the Galveston Gas Company (the first in Texas), Galveston Bagging & Cordage Company, and Brush Electric Light & Power Company (the first in Texas); and chaired the committee that built the city's waterworks. He remained nominal president of the family hardware business managed by son John Stoddart Brown. He was also president of the powerful Galveston Wharf Company, where he was finally able to effect improvements he had long advocated; as a result of his labors, Galveston became the only deepwater port on the Gulf of Mexico between New Orleans and Vera Cruz. Brown was a director of the Union & Marine Fire Insurance Company and "other corporations of character and standing," including the Life Association of America (Galveston Board).

9    *Opera Glass*, May 24, 1885.

10   Information on Waukesha from: Charlotte Reid Seybold, "Resort Attracted Texas Beauty," no attribution, September 18, 1953; same, "Interesting Guests at Fountain Spring House," *Waukesha Daily Freeman*, nd; and

*Milwaukee Journal*, March 9, 1930, all courtesy of Waukesha County Museum.

11  *Ibid.*

12  The Adirondacks became popular in the 1870s. Soon after the conclusion of the Civil War, newspaper manufacturers began to substitute wood pulp for rags, which stimulated lumbering throughout the country, including the Adirondacks. After rail lines were built into the mountains to haul out timber, visitors quickly followed.

Childwold Park had an office on Fifth Avenue in New York City. Visitors boarded the Adirondack & St. Lawrence branch of the New York Central & Hudson Railroad for the journey to the park's station, then endured a bumpy six-mile carriage ride to the facility. The hotel accommodated over 200 people and was eventually expanded to hold 100 more. Among the guests who stayed there were several presidents of the United States.

Childwold Park closed at the end of the 1909 season after it became apparent it could not survive the impact of the "rich man's panic" of 1907; it eventually became a private preserve. (Information courtesy of The Adirondack Museum in Blue Mountain Lake, New York.)

13  The Empire was rebuilt in 1923 and still operates as a hotel adjacent to Lincoln Center. Quotation from brochure on hotel, courtesy New York Historical Society.

14  Copying the works of masters was an accepted form of art study.

15  Still a third variation shows a winged cupid kissing a woman; today it is in a private collection.

16  Information about the Texas Women's World's Fair Association is amazingly scant; the author could find no extant records, and few people had even heard of the organization.

According to a small pamphlet issued by Mrs. Tobin, each county or senatorial district had a committee which raised and turned in funds to the Board of Lady Managers through their treasurer in Waco; the Board was also given an office in the Capitol building for headquarters, which gave the ladies quasi-state approval.

Bettie's personal copy of the *Guide to the World's Fair* is on display in *Ashton Villa*. Sources for this section:

Mrs. W. H. Tobin, "To the Women of Texas," an undated pamphlet

Edward Hake Phillips, "Texas and the World Fairs, 1851-1935," *East Texas Historical Journal*

*History of Texas Together with a Biographical History of the Cities of Houston and Galveston*, 1893.

17  Moreau's first wife, Alice Jane Daugherty Brown, died in Galveston of tuberculosis in 1884. Two years later he married Louise Grevenberg of Louisiana; Moreau and Louise had one child, Rebecca Alice (later changed to Rebekah), born in 1895.

After a successful medical career in Galveston, Moreau moved to Chicago, Illinois in the mid-1880s and "accepted the position of professor of laryngology and rhinology at the Chicago Polyclinic and the College of Physicians and Surgeons of Chicago." (Hafertepe, page 29)

18  Maude Elliott Howe, *Art and Handicraft in the Woman's Building of the World's Columbian Exposition, Chicago, 1893*, preface, page 23.

# CHAPTER FIVE

# Turmoil in the Family

After the pleasurable years that had preceded it, the mid-1890s were marked by significant turmoil and pain for Bettie and her family.

## A CHRISTMAS DEATH

Late in 1894 James Brown began to suffer ill health; doctors soon diagnosed his condition as epithelial cancer, commonly known today as carcinoma. The following February, Bettie and Moreau took him north in search of treatment, "hoping to stay the disease." Spring found Bettie and her father in Patterson, New Jersey, and by summer they were staying in an "apartment house" in New York City.[1] They were not bereft of family the entire time; Moreau came regularly, and Matilda, Thomas, and the children visited them in New Jersey. But all medical efforts were unsuccessful, and Bettie and her father returned to *Ashton Villa* in October.

James Moreau Brown died in the house he had built and surrounded by his family sometime during the night of December 24-25, 1895 at the age of 74.[2] Among the pallbearers who participated in the funeral at Trinity Episcopal Church were some of the most influential people in Texas business circles, including Colonel W. L. Moody, George Sealy, J. H. Hutchings, Henry Sealy, and William M. Rice.[3] Brown was buried in the Episcopal Cemetery in accordance with the rites of the Knights Templar, of which he had been Galveston's oldest member.

Many newspapers and magazines eulogized him. Perhaps the best summation of James Brown's career is found in the *Historical Review of South-East Texas* (1910). He was "one of the most eminent business men and citizens of Texas . . . His remarkable executive ability made him a creator of enterprise while others were workers, and for this reason his name is the most conspicuous of those identified with the promotion and upbuilding of several enterprises which are part of the foundation of Galveston's greatness."

His estate went in its entirety to wife Rebecca, who was named his administrator. James had already conveyed to her most of his real estate holdings in July of 1893 "to belong to her as her Seperate [sic] Estate." But these deeds were not filed with the Galveston County Clerk's Office until the end of 1894 when his illness became apparent. Likely, the doctors had told him the cancer was fatal, and he wanted to keep his valuable land holdings out of the estate, where they would be taxed.

James Brown's will is very brief and stipulated that his estate was "to be administered without the jurisdiction or proceedings of any Court and that no action be had in the County Court or any Court . . . other than the proving and recording of this will."[4] Accordingly, there is no inventory to list the size and contents of his holdings. The reason for this action is not clear; perhaps he didn't want taxing authorities to know what he owned, perhaps he simply didn't like people nosing into the fortune he'd worked years to build.

Her father's death and the long months she had spent in caring for him must have devastated Bettie. But even more troubles were on their way.

## A TROUBLED MARRIAGE

Even before Mr. Brown's illness, signs of stress had become visible in Matilda's marriage. Since her marriage to Thomas in 1884, Matilda had borne three children: Moreau Brown, or Maury (Morey) (1885), Charles James, called C. J. by the family (1888), and Matilda Alice, simply known as Alice (1890).

Thomas began drinking heavily early in their marriage. Bettie apparently became aware of the problem when Maury was only three weeks old. She had met her sister and brother-in-law at the Beach Hotel, Galveston's first major resort hotel, which had opened in 1883. Thomas "went to see me [that is, escort her] to the elevator and I had to hold him up and see him back again to the room where Mrs. Sweeney was rocking the cradle and crying."[5] Later, when C. J. and then Alice were born, Bettie stayed at the Sweeneys' house to help care for Matilda and was forced to listen to the "profane language" Thomas used with her sister.

In 1893 Matilda became seriously ill with pleurisy, and Bettie moved in to nurse her younger sister, only to see the profanity and drinking repeat itself. "Mr. Sweeney," said his sister-in-law severely, "was either drunk or under some strange and evil influence. . . ." At one point, she recalled, she entered Matilda's room to find Thomas trying to help his wife sit upright; when she went to his aid, Thomas cursed her. "Damn it all[,] get out of here." He then began weaving about, fell and hit his head on the bureau and knocked himself unconscious.

As the years passed, Thomas' drinking became heavier and more public. At first, he was careful that no one witnessed his tirades, paying off the servants at his own home and even at *Ashton Villa* to leave the room before he exploded. But the servants were loyal to Matilda and disgusted that the master would pass out anywhere in the house: they simply left him where he fell to "sleep it off." Thomas appeared at *Ashton*

*Villa* drunk more than once and even tried to enter Bettie's room. Several times he traveled north to New York only to behave in the same way. Bettie lunched with him one day in that city but "was mortified by his drinking and loud and boisterous behavior."

When later questioned about her relationship with her brother-in-law, she admitted that Thomas had indeed once come to visit her in the Adirondacks when she was sick. And he "treated me with as much kindness as he could, considering the fact that he was 'under the influence' the whole time." Mr. Sweeney, she concluded distastefully, brought her a fan and left her his bar bill to pay.

Thomas abused Matilda both physically and with words, and he so frightened the children that they would escape to the kitchen or lock themselves in their rooms. His wife's response was passive: she cried, fled to her own room, or tried to pretend that he was merely ill. Finally, when his behavior became too aggressive, the gentle Matilda simply stopped receiving visitors—even her own family—for fear of what Thomas would do or say.

## FLEEING HOME

In December of 1894 Matilda and the children were forced to flee their home for the first time when Thomas became so violent that she took them to *Ashton Villa*. Her concern was natural since he had several times fired off a pistol in his bedroom while threatening to shoot himself.

Her brother Charles Rhodes Brown had married Estelle Austin,[6] a schoolmate of Matilda's, in 1890, and they lived just behind the Sweeneys on Avenue K. On a second occasion, in January of 1895, Matilda and the three children, still dressed in their nightclothes, ran to Charles' house, bolted up the stairs, and locked themselves in Estelle's bedroom, nine-year-old Maury standing against the door for good measure. After Estelle refused to open the door to her brother-in-law and he left, Matilda took the children to *Ashton Villa*. Charles stayed the night with a distraught Thomas, then went himself to *Ashton Villa* the next day to persuade his sister to return home. The scenario was repeated in February, and this time an ill James Brown intervened, begging Matilda to divorce Thomas and come home. But she "refused to do so on account of their children and to avoid, if possible, the publicity and notoriety of suit. . . ."

## ORIGIN OF TALES?

As might be supposed, Bettie did not much care for Thomas Sweeney; and he returned the favor. Nor was their mutual dislike of recent origin but, apparently, dated back some years. Thomas had been "paying attention" to a woman and wanted Bettie to take her out (that is, to recognize her socially) but she refused. He threatened to ruin her name, and Bettie called in her father, who "settled the question" in an unspecified way. Neither she nor Thomas ever spoke of the matter again, and Bettie said she had "buried the hatchet and thought he had done the same."

But later in her testimony she added that Thomas had threatened to keep her sister from her if she, Bettie, "did not take the woman out as he requested." That would indicate that his relationship with the unknown woman lasted some time, presumably while James Brown was too ill to stop the affair and continuing after his death. One wonders why James' sons did not intercede on their sister's behalf.[7]

The fastidious Bettie was offended by her brother-in-law's messy drunkenness. "I have seen him often on the street apparently sober and then seen him at home shortly afterwards lying on the lounge with and [sic] empty bottle in his arms and too drunk to move, and the air of the room offensively strong with the fumes of whiskey." Though she felt he was a "rough diamond," Bettie reported politely, she tried to accept Thomas for Matilda's sake and did all she could "to make him mend his ways."

But Thomas was not grateful for that help. Instead, he developed a near hatred of Bettie.

The Sweeneys' neighbor Rowena Spillane later testified that "it was habitual with him when drunk to abuse Miss Betty . . . it seemed to be a mania with him to abuse [her] by inuendo [sic]." He came to blame her for the problems with his marriage and declared to Mrs. Spillane that he would have his revenge on his sister-in-law and "would bring her proud head down to the dust." He then concluded by telling her "he could tell a tale on Miss Betty Brown that would make my hair stand on end."

These reports lead one to question whether Thomas Sweeney was not, in fact, the origin of some of the more interesting, if not scurrilous, tales about Bettie.

## BREAKUP OF THE MARRIAGE

Sometime in 1895 Matilda finally persuaded her husband to enter "a sanatarium [sic] for such cases" and even went with him to support him. But the treatment failed.

A week after James Brown died, Thomas again "became so outrageous" that Matilda and the children once more fled to *Ashton Villa*, this time with the intention of staying away. Thomas followed her there, but his wife, Bettie testified, locked herself in the east second-floor bathroom and refused to see him. He finally left but returned in ten minutes, still intent on talking to Matilda. When Bettie confronted him, Thomas grabbed a nearby doorframe to hold himself up and "trying to shake his fist at me he went into such a volley of incoherent talk I could not understand any intelligence in it: and he finally staggered off and that was the last conversation I ever had with him."

Matilda consulted with her attorney and with Thomas' priest and, in the end, sent word that she would file for divorce unless he stayed away and desisted "in his cruel treatment for such a time as would warrant her in believing that he could and would" behave himself. He promised and Matilda allowed herself to be talked into going home, but the truce only lasted a few days. On the first of February, 1896, he threatened her with a carving knife. She went back to *Ashton Villa*, and Thomas left Galveston with the intention of going to Europe to live; he got as far as New York.

Matilda filed for divorce in April. Her petition declared that she "was tenderly raised in wealth and luxury, and educated as became her station in life, and is of refined sensibilities and a lady of culture." Her husband, she averred, had been unfaithful for seven years and had caused her "a degree of mental distress which threatened to impair her mind and health." Moreover, Thomas' drinking had led him to neglect his business so badly that she'd been forced to support them from her own property and with James Brown's assistance, while he was alive.

Interestingly, Matilda's petition also stated her belief that her husband's problems were "largely owing to his being constantly and habitually under the influence of an outsider and of liquor or some drug," but does not name this "outsider."

Thomas, meanwhile, had returned to Galveston, broken into their house, and "taken possession" of it while Matilda was living at *Ashton Villa*. She promptly obtained an injunction to keep him or anyone associated with him from trespassing in their house and requiring him to vacate it. He denied all the allegations in her divorce petition and quickly got into property issues. Matilda had claimed that Lot 8, Block 84 belonged to her, it and the house being a wedding present from her parents. Thomas countered that the land was hers but not the house or furnishings, which had cost $12,000 and were paid for out of their community estate and with money he'd earned. He also requested custody of the boys—not Alice—"that they may be properly prepared and fitted for the duties of life and citizenship."

Thomas blamed his business problems on "the stringency of the times and the commercial depression all over the world" and insinuated that Matilda had filed for divorce, not because she wanted to, but because other people, *i.e.*, Bettie, had pushed her into it. That was a theme he would sound over and over again during the messy months of trial proceedings that followed.

## ATTACK ON MRS. BROWN

Mrs. J. M. Brown had also come in for her share of abuse from her son-in-law, beginning in 1889 when he drunkenly insisted that she invite a young San Antonio woman he knew to visit her. Not only did she refuse but the redoubtable Mrs. Brown wrote "a letter of advice" to the woman in question which Thomas eventually obtained and became angry over.

During the depositions made as part of Matilda's divorce hearing, Mrs. Brown answered the questions put to her calmly but without much elaboration and refuted Thomas' claims that he squired her to many social events. When asked if he had not always been kind and generous to her, she replied succinctly, "Not always." His attorneys pounded on the theme that the Browns wanted to get rid of Thomas because he was broke—"the high and exalted purpose that animates you and every one of your family"—but Mrs. Brown countered that "money or want of money has nothing to do with it."

By the time they reached their twelfth and last question, snidely inquiring whether the Browns had ever had any definite social standing until Sweeney married into it, Rebecca Ashton

Stoddart Brown was getting testy. "I can't say," she replied aloofly, "that is a matter of opinion for the community where we live to pronounce."

## LIGHT SHED ON BETTIE

The material record of the Sweeneys' divorce is as sad as any. Hidden within it, however, are gems of information about Bettie not found anyplace else, since no letters or diaries of hers have survived or yet surfaced.

In the first place, and as might be expected, she became quite involved in helping her sister, speaking to potential witnesses and giving her own lengthy deposition. She undoubtedly supported her mother, too, in what must have been an extremely unpleasant experience.

Secondly, it is interesting to note that even Thomas Sweeney's attorneys acknowledged Bettie's social prowess by asking her to confirm that she was "generally known by the name of Miss Betty Brown in Galveston, San Antonio, Chicago, Waukesha, and New York," indicating that all were places she traveled to regularly and where she was well known.[8]

Bettie's pride in being a Brown of Galveston and her father's daughter surfaced in a very pointed way. Sweeney's attorneys asked her about a particular matter and then commanded, "Be specific and remember that you are under oath to tell the truth." One can only imagine how she must have straightened up even more, her blue eyes fiery as she answered: "It is not necessary for Mr. J. M. Brown's daughter to be reminded to tell the truth." When belabored to acknowledge that she had happily introduced Thomas as a brother, she snapped, "I have never introduced any one except my own brothers with pride or happiness as a brother . . . [I] . . . was *accustomed* to introducing him as my brotherinlaw [*sic*]."

That she had been deeply worried about her sister and unable to do anything about it must have been galling. One night, someone had called *Ashton Villa* to report a disturbance at the Sweeneys' house, and Bettie had gone herself to check out the matter. In the dark, she stood outside on the sidewalk "looking and listening to see what was the matter." Thomas was vilely cursing his wife, but Matilda remained silent. For a few long moments, Bettie actually feared he had killed her, until she saw Matilda moving about. If she then entered the house to intercede, she did not report it in her testimony; but it is difficult to see her simply walking away.

The picture that emerges from her testimony is of a woman undeniably proud of her origins, protective of her family, and disgusted by the sordid. In contrast to her mother's brief answers, Bettie responded fully and directly, not hesitating to take up the cudgels against Sweeney's unfriendly lawyers who attempted to make her the sinister, driving force behind Matilda's filing for divorce.

"Is it not true," they demanded, "that Mrs. Sweeney is under the hypnotic influence of yourself and the balance of your family. . .?" To which Bettie responded tartly, "If I had ever possessed any hypnotic power I should have used it on Mr. Sweeney to make him a good husband to my sister whom I idolized. Our family have [sic] done everything in their power to make him a good man and devoted husband, and to smoth [sic] over the difficulties he has made with his wife. We have tried this for years; but some unseen power seems to have possessed him[,] rendering her life with him longer unendurable."

## END OF THE ORDEAL

When all the testimony was over, more than seven months after her original petition was filed, the court ruled in Matilda's favor, granting her a divorce, custody of her children, and ownership of the house and property. Thomas received "control and education" of the two boys, although the court required them to live with their mother when they were not in boarding school. With Maury, C. J., and Alice, Matilda moved back home to *Ashton Villa* where she raised her family with the help of her mother and sister. Galveston may have whispered about what a shocking thing it had been, but few who knew the real story could have blamed the gently bred Matilda for taking such a step. Divorce wasn't at all unheard of in her circles, but the elite still looked askance—not at the action itself, but at the notoriety that accompanied it.[9] Thomas vacated the house on Avenue L, which Matilda finally sold in 1905, and he lived thereafter in various downtown hotels, including the Tremont House.

Matilda lived the rest of her years fairly quietly. Perhaps she did so in an attempt to live down the scandal, and perhaps that was simply what she'd wanted all along.

And what effect did her trials have on Bettie? The divorce following hard on the heels of her beloved father's death must have caused her to step back and take a look at her own life. But it would take a literal act of God to change the redoubtable Miss Bettie.

## Notes: Chapter Five

1  Affidavit dated July 24, 1896 and given by Bettie in the course of Matilda Brown Sweeney's divorce proceedings; Case #18027 on file in District Clerk's Office, Galveston County Courthouse. All subsequent quotes from Bettie in this chapter are from same source.

2  Moreau arrived from Chicago "just in time to see his father, Mr. J. M. Brown, previous to his death. . . ." (The *Opera Glass*, December 28, 1895.) The *Opera Glass* gave the time of his death as 10 a.m. Christmas (Wednesday) morning, but the *Galveston Daily News* reported it occurred "Tuesday night."

3  Moody was the patriarch of the family that made its fortune in cotton and banking; the Galveston house his son W. L. Jr. bought from the heirs of R. S. and Narcissa Willis is now the Moody Mansion and Museum. His son W. L. Jr. and granddaughter Mary Moody Northen established charitable foundations which have been prominent in Texas. Hutchings was prominent in railroads and real estate and was a banking partner with John Sealy (Hutchings-Sealy Bank). William Marsh Rice of Houston made his first fortune on the "Cotton Road" from Texas to Mexico during the Civil War; that is likely where he made James Brown's acquaintance. Rice later moved to New York City, where he was murdered in 1896; his $3 million estate founded Rice University in Houston.

   James Brown's obituary also mentions his long and close friendship with A(lexander) T(urney) Stewart: "His [Brown's] relations in New York and his successful business enterprises widened the scope of his acquaintance and brought him in touch with many leading men of the country . . . he never went to New York without calling on the merchant-prince [Stewart], with whom he enjoyed an intimate acquaintance." The Irish-born Stewart (1803-1876) made his first fortune by investing in Irish lace and opening a store on Broadway in New York City. By 1862 his operation covered an entire city block and was housed in an eight-story building. Stewart owned factories in both New York and Europe, built Garden City on Long Island and two hotels at Saratoga, and was reputed to be worth $40 to $50 million at his death. A surviving piece of stationery from J. S. Brown Hardware Company notes that the firm had an office in the Stewart building in 1898.

4   Galveston County Probate Records, Book 30, page 560.

5   All descriptions of Thomas Sweeney's behavior are taken from various affidavits filed during Matilda's divorce proceedings; see note 1.

6   Estelle was the daughter of Edward T. Austin and the granddaughter of Captain Henry Austin, first cousin of Texas founder Stephen F. Austin. Henry's sister Mary Austin Holley wrote one of the first Anglo histories of Texas.

Charles led an adventurous life before settling down and getting married. After studying art in Europe, he entered the family hardware business but left after three years and moved to California. He was a sailor for a while, then moved to San Angelo, Texas, where he ranched and met Estelle. They married there on June 3, 1891, with Reba McClanahan and Rebecca Brown (Mrs. J. M.) among the guests who traveled out from Galveston. When the couple returned to Galveston in 1892, he became a life insurance agent. He and Estelle had seven children: Lydia Estelle (1891), Rebecca Austin (189?), Matilda Stoddart (1895), James Taylor (1896), Adele Herbert (1900), Elizabeth Constance (1903), and Estelle Rose (1905).

7   Oddly, neither of Matilda's Galveston brothers seems to have testified or been in any way involved in her suit. Estelle Brown, Charles' wife, was deposed, as was Mrs.

Brown, Bettie, a number of servants at both houses, a nurse, and a neighbor. But neither Charles nor John appear in the records.

8    Bettie replied that she had many pet names among her friends, "Betty" being one of them. Research indicates that most friends and acquaintances spelled her name that way, rather than with the "ie" she favored.

9    "Divorces were much more common in the late nineteenth century than we think. Divorces increased 15 percent in Victorian America, making the United States the country with the highest divorce rate in the world by 1915. One out of seven marriages failed. . . . Under pressure for marital reform, divorce became somewhat more accessible to women towards the end of the century, although the divorced woman continued to suffer from a greater social stigma than her ex-husband. Nevertheless, divorce remained largely a privilege of the upper classes and, for the most part, it remained entirely a male prerogative." (From *Ashton Villa Docent's Manual*, compiled by Beth Anne Weidler, curator.)

About the time Matilda's divorce was granted, the family received another blow when John T. McClanahan, the young husband of John Stoddart Brown's daughter Rebecca Ashton—"Reba"—died suddenly. Reba and John, a druggist, had married in 1890 and lived just a few blocks from both her father's home *Live Oak Terrace* and from *Ashton Villa*. After his death, she returned with her son John McClanahan Jr. to *Live Oak Terrace*. In 1898 Reba (1874-1950) married again; William P. Gaines was the founder of the *Austin American-Statesman*.

# CHAPTER SIX

# That Terrible September

The return to *Ashton Villa* of the Sweeney family necessitated changes to the house that Bettie undoubtedly took up with great delight. And for a few years after Mr. Brown's death, they enjoyed a peaceful life.

## THE LAST REMODELING

*Ashton Villa* had been built symmetrically in a great square block, unlike most residential Italianate structures which featured interesting shapes and asymmetrical facades. Now at last, it would assume a similar design.

Under Bettie's direction, a semi-octagonal wing was added to the east side of the house in 1899 that was three stories tall. To build it, workers tore down the frame and glass conservatory that had been added during the 1870s remodeling.

The additional space produced in the dining room allowed the Brown ladies to seat many more guests at formal dinners. Upstairs, the new wing let Alice and her mother Matilda share the northeast bedroom that had previously served as Mr. and Mrs. Brown's sitting room. The Sweeney boys had rooms on the third floor, as had their uncles before them. Also on the third floor, material from the old conservatory was used to create in the new wing what has popularly been known as Bettie's art studio.[1]

Mrs. Brown's mother, Sarah Warner Moses Stoddart Rhodes, widowed now for the second time, maintained an apartment adjacent to the studio. "Mere," as the family called her, "was a woman of 'spunk' and independence, ruling all who came under her hand," according to her great-granddaughter, Rebecca Slack. Her health remained remarkable even into her nineties—she refused to use a cane and never wore spectacles—and she continued to climb the steps to her apartment every day, scorning the installation of an elevator.[2] Family members must have seen many echoes of this pioneer woman in her granddaughter Bettie.

## LIFE AT ASHTON VILLA

The ladies of *Ashton Villa* then settled back to enjoy a social life similar to what they'd had before the personal traumas of the mid-'90s and the several national financial panics that also marked the period.

It is to Alice Sweeney Jumonville, Matilda's daughter, and to Rebekah Brown Allgeyer, Moreau's daughter, that we owe much of our knowledge of these years. Just a child when her family moved back to *Ashton Villa*, Alice grew to young womanhood in the house and retained vivid memories of life there. Rebekah, or Becky as she was called, visited Grandmother and Aunt Bettie regularly and also wrote many reminiscences.

Mrs. Brown was an affable, plump figure always dressed in black taffeta silk and surrounded by as many grandchildren as possible. She wore a "mop-cap" on her white hair, and her favorite spot was a rocking chair in the family room, from which she dispensed instructions to the servants every morning. She traveled some, visiting Austin, for example, in the early winter of 1897 with Matilda and daughter-in-law Helen Brown (John's wife).[3] A few weeks later she and Bettie attended a reception given by the Mallory Steamship Lines, and in the spring of 1898 she allowed Bettie to throw a party for 300 guests at *Ashton Villa*, over which her daughter presided "with queenly grace."[4] She described herself as a landlord on the 1900 Census, a reference to the real estate holdings, many of them rental properties, which James Brown had left her. However, oldest son John Stoddart actually managed the business details.

In happier times, the Brown family gathered to celebrate the engagement of John Stoddart Brown's daughter, Reba, to J. T. McClanahan. Left to right: Rebecca Ashton Stoddart Brown, J. Moreau Brown Jr. (Moreau's son), Reba, Edgene Brown (John's daughter), John Stoddart Brown, his wife Helen, John McClanahan, Helen Brown (John's daughter), Bettie (holding glass), James Moreau Brown, Thomas H. Sweeney, and Matilda Brown Sweeney holding son C. J. (Courtesy of Rosenberg Library, Galveston, Texas)

At some point, Mrs. Brown also became interested in the Letitia Rosenberg Woman's Home, which was organized in 1889 to care for indigent older women. The extent of her involvement is not clear, but her generosity to the cause must have been outstanding, for *Ashton Villa* came to be filled with many examples of embroidered linenwork executed by the Home's residents and given to Mrs. Brown—and later to Bettie—in gratitude.

## KITTENS ON HER TRAIN

But it was Aunt Bettie who captured the children's imaginations. Fun, spirited, a little bit shocking, she must have been an ideal aunt.

Bettie's beloved Angora cats continued to wander the house, and the youngsters remembered with glee that she would place several of the ever-present kittens on the long trains she affected on her dresses and ride them around. "I have NEVER seen my Aunt Betty with out [sic] a train, even [on] her pinoirs [peignoirs] and night gowns," recalled Becky Allgeyer, Moreau's daughter. Her blonde hair was always "held in place with gold hair pins. She had many sets, a set [of pins] to match each and every set of the jewelry she wore[,] pearls, diamonds, rubies, emeralds, etc." Mrs. Allgeyer, in fact, had a good laugh when she visited *Ashton Villa* after its restoration as a museum and was told by the docent that a small floor safe in the dining room was where the family silver was kept. "I could not contain my mirth and loudly proclaimed, 'This safe could not contain my Aunt Betty's jewels, much less the family silver.'"[5]

Alice recalled that her aunt "was a very beautiful, talented and fascinating woman at all times . . . tall, of beautiful figure, queenly dignity and graciousness personified." Becky's memories were a bit less diplomatic in some respects. "She was not a raving beauty but held herself erect—head high & her grecian nose always seemed as tho' she was smelling something—

either good or bad . . . she was a queen tho' she was not a beauty. She carried herself so erectly and gave one the feeling they were in the presence of royalty. When she rode in her open carriage which was drawn by 2 white horses and the top folded back, Aunt Betty had a real lace parasol which she carried & which matched the color of her gown."

To sustain her between periodic trips to Europe, Bettie was active in Galveston's cultural life, with memberships in several literary societies and the Ladies Musical Club.

## BETTIE ENTERTAINS

Sublimely disregarding changing economic conditions in the world, Bettie led her family back to the "old days," when *Ashton Villa* was the center of Galveston hospitality and every event was a lavish one . . . although the younger Browns and Sweeneys didn't particularly share Aunt Bettie's taste for the formal.

"Christmas dinner at Grandma's was a bore," one of Charles' children recalled bluntly. On such formal occasions, the members of the younger generation took their meal in the dining room of the main house, rather than in the family room. And while they had their own separate table, the children were required to stay through most of the dinner, a process that could last three or four hours. A line of servants dressed in "the house livery of sapphire blue and silver satin" passed around dozens of gleaming silver trays and bowls, while the table was filled with porcelain, cut crystal, and more silver.

Charles' daughter Lydia Estelle Hanna described one such occasion: "In the center [of the table] was an epergne filled with fruit and flowers, and by each plate was a small dish of salted almonds. I was told that the epergne, a porcelain affair decorated with cupids, flowers, etc. was a gift to Aunt Bettie from an old beau, Nichols Stuart.

"The first course was oysters on the half-shell, served on plates set in crushed ice; oyster stew followed. Next, huge silver salvers with domed lids were brought in with great pomp; on one, a roasted pig with an apple in its mouth; on the other, an enormous turkey. These were carved at the sideboard and then served around the table. Vegetables were next brought around . . .

"Soon after this all the youngsters were politely but firmly excused . . . so we played outside with our toys until called back for dessert. We watched with little interest while a flaming plum-pudding with brandied hard sauce made its adult rounds; then came *our* dessert! A large silver platter with a nest of spun sugar and in the center a life-sized ice cream hen, surrounded by yellow ice-cream baby chicks, one for each child, all frozen hard as rocks. This dessert was an exclusive of the Brown house, as the moulds were made in New York for Aunt Bettie, and as far as I know no one else was allowed to use them. Mr. Kahn, the owner of 'The Confectionary,' molded the ice cream and made the spun sugar."

## INDULGING THE CHILDREN

With no children of her own, Bettie proved an indulgent aunt to her nieces and nephews as well as to other neighborhood children. To Mary Moody, daughter of the wealthy W. L. Moody Jr. who lived just a few blocks up Broadway, Bettie lent a gypsy outfit for a party, actually a folk costume she'd bought on one of her many trips abroad. She took niece Rebekah Brown (Allgeyer) of Chicago to Marshall Field's after the little girl bravely endured a tooth-pulling. "I did not cry so she took me across the street . . . & I selected a beautiful doll dressed in white with gold threads and brilliants on her lovely dress & a red velvet train, bordered in ermine, a jeweled crown on her head & a small real diamond ring which was tied onto the doll[']s wrist with white satin ribbon & the ring just fit me."

Decades later, the memory of that wonderful doll remained fresh in Rebekah's memory.

Several descendants still cherish delicate and expensive porcelain dolls purchased in Europe by Aunt Bettie and brought back to Galveston. One was christened "Miss Bettie" for its blonde pompadour hairstyle and turquoise velvet dress—Bettie's signature color. Another was "Buster Brown" with reddish-brown hair fixed in a Dutch bob. Both were gifts to Charles Rhodes' daughter Rebecca Austin Brown.

## PARTYING WITH ROYALTY

Sometime between 1898 and the summer of 1900, Bettie returned to Europe once more.[6] While there, she attended a "lawn tea party at the Castle in Austria where Prince Joseph was in residence."[7] For this occasion, she splurged on a fabulous costume that cost her every penny of $5,000. Over a sapphire-blue gown with a modest bustle, Bettie wore a white full-length, trained coat heavily embellished with lace and what appear to be Fortuny-style pleats at the collar and cuffs. On her head was a straw hat decorated with velvet bows and silk flowers to match. Completing the ensemble were a parasol to match, lace fan, diamond stud earrings, pearl choker, diamond necklace, several rings, and a gold chain belt.

This coat was reputed to have remained in the family until it was lost in a 1947 hurricane in Mississippi.

But Bettie's most amazing trip must be the one she made to Japan, not an easy destination to reach in our own time and surely fraught with adventure in her day. Unfortunately, very little information has survived from it. Even the date is in question; research failed to turn up anything more conclusive than that she traveled there sometime between 1893 and 1912. Several items which still remain in the possession of descendants were likely purchased in Japan: an Oriental vase

Here, Bettie wears her famous $5,000 lace coat and sapphire gown, purchased for a garden party at one of the imperial Austrian residences. (Courtesy *Ashton Villa*)

This portrait of Bettie was made by the A. F. Bradley Studio in New York City sometime between 1898 and 1901. (Courtesy *Ashton Villa*)

that stood on the mantel of Bettie's bedroom, a tiny, exquisitely carved ivory elephant, and—her favorite collectible—fans.

## DEVASTATION FROM THE SEA

The Browns' idyllic life continued for several years until the tragic events of September 8 and 9, 1900.

That was the date of "The Great Storm," a massive hurricane that slammed into Galveston from the Gulf of Mexico and nearly destroyed the Queen City. Warning signs of an impending storm had been evident for several days, but city residents were accustomed to bad weather and took no unusual precautions. Even when the surf became too rough for swimming on September 7, few people realized the significance.

Early on the morning of the eighth, the main body of the hurricane reached the island, and by mid-afternoon, much of Galveston was under water. Wind speeds reached an estimated 120 miles per hour, and a four-foot storm surge caused by a sudden shift in those winds wiped clean most of the city's south and east sides. At its highest point, flood waters reached nearly sixteen feet high.

And when the winds and the rains finally ceased, more than 6,000 people on the island—16 percent of the population— were dead.[8] Nearly a century later, the 1900 Storm is still the worst natural disaster to have ever hit the United States.

The inhabitants of *Ashton Villa* fared better than most for several reasons. The house had been built on the island's highest point, a ridge about seven or eight feet above the average level of low tide. In addition, the storm surge pushed inland a mighty pile of debris four to ten feet high—composed mostly of the remnants of wooden houses from the beachfront—that stopped only a few blocks from *Ashton Villa*. That provided the house a buffer against the most destructive force of the surge. And because it had a raised basement, the

Brown's home was flooded only to a height of about six feet on the first floor. It did suffer serious damage to the roof from the winds, and most of the massive oak trees that had once adorned the grounds were uprooted.

Ten-year-old Alice Sweeney (Jumonville) told her family later that she was ordered to sit quietly on the hall staircase while Bettie and Matilda took all the cut glass and china out of the cabinets and sat them on the floor. Other valuables that could be carried were moved to the upper floors. And as the water advanced into the house, Alice would move up a step: she made it to the tenth step before the water stopped rising. *Ashton Villa* was nearly full with Bettie, Mrs. Brown, Mrs. Stoddart, and Matilda and her children as well as Charles Rhodes Brown's family, including baby Adele, just two days old.

## AFTERMATH

When the rains stopped, Bettie and her family emerged to inspect the damage. The first floor was filled with silt and mud; remarkably, when that was cleaned away, most of the china and crystal was found unbroken. Large furniture that had to be left in place was ruined by the water, as were the floors and carpets; the roof was damaged (especially on the newly completed addition); and windows were broken. The yard was littered with uprooted trees and debris that floated in from everywhere. Among the salvage left there, family members say, were two armoires that were never claimed. Bettie later sketched a design for a new sideboard for the dining room (presumably, the old one was destroyed by flood waters) using these two pieces of furniture for inspiration.

By far the most serious problem was safe drinking water. The two main cisterns in the cellar had been contaminated with salt water, and only the small cistern on the roof was still fresh. Drinking water was in short supply all through the city.

Soon the house began to fill with refugees who needed food and clothes, among them Alexander and Stanley Spencer, whose mother was a friend of Mrs. Brown's. Their father was killed in the storm, and Mrs. Brown sent for the children and their mother to come to *Ashton Villa*.[9] The boys feared they would have to give up their pet lamb for food, but from somewhere, the Browns obtained a calf which they killed and cleaned, Bettie and Matilda cutting up the animal themselves. That provided food for several days. And when the fresh water was gone, they "had to beg it from the neighbors." Bettie, her sister, and her mother scraped together what food they could find and carried baskets to other houses where people were in need.

Larry Chittendon, a New York poet, wrote this about Bettie's efforts after the storm:

> *"When storm winds wrecked the city, blew hard*
>   *about the town,*
> *The first to house the homeless was Miss Rebecca*
>   *Brown.*
> *She and her gentle sister - the kindly "Mrs. S -"*
> *Led all the queens of fashion through suffering and*
>   *distress.*
> *They gave out food and money, and with their jeweled*
>   *hands,*
> *They toiled and worked like heroes for sorrow-stricken*
>   *bands. . . ."*[10]

A bit flowery in its sentiments, but the essence of the poem was that the sophisticated Miss Rebecca Brown, collector of clothes and jewelry, got her hands very dirty in helping her beloved Galveston to recover. And it was a task that would consume many years.

Tons of debris had to be cleared away . . . houses, dead animals, and human remains. A few days in the September heat, and bodies began to swell and turn black. The odor was horrific, not just from flesh but also from decaying organic material such as trees and other plants. The city was covered with a pall of smoke from burning all this debris.[11] There was no electricity, little, water, and a great deal of looting. The mental effect on the residents could be seen in either blank faces or laughing, joking references to the number of family and friends who had died: the loss was simply too great for their emotions to cope with.

For the Browns, who had watched Galveston rise from a tiny village to become the elegant "Queen City of the Gulf," this devastation must have been heartwrenching beyond belief.

To avoid such a horror happening again, the city decided to undertake a monumental project: building a raised seawall along the southern oceanfront exposure. Behind the wall, structures were jacked up and filled in beneath to raise the entire city to a higher level.[12] *Ashton Villa* did not require raising since it was already at the island's highest point, but the yard was filled with sand to even the grade. That meant the loss of the basement and the lower two-to-three feet of the iron fence around the property, which is still half-buried to this day.[13]

## A SOBER MISS BETTIE

What impact did the 1900 Storm have on Bettie?

While none of the Brown family died, due to the elevated location of their homes along and just off Broadway, they did lose friends and acquaintances. Long known landmarks were gone or so damaged they had to be demolished—Sacred Heart Church, City Hall, the Orphan's Home, the waterworks that James Brown had helped build, and so many others. Only those who have been through a similar natural disaster can understand the emotional trauma, the feelings of guilt, of experiencing something so deadly—and of surviving it when many others do not.[14]

Combined with the family's personal troubles of the preceding decade, the Great 1900 Storm was enough to sober even a Bettie Brown. And over the next few years, she would take up a very different course to her life.

## Notes: Chapter Six

1   The author questions whether the room was ever actually used for this purpose. It would not appear to have had enough natural light to serve as a studio. And to reach it, Bettie would have had to cross through an occupied bedroom.

The third floor of *Ashton Villa* is one of the few places where one can gain an impression of what the house looked like when it was first built in 1859. Simple, arched fireplace surrounds were painted in a faux marble design. Over each Italianate rounded arch window—the shortest on the house—a plain lintel is set into the wall to imitate the facade design. No photographs of this floor exist, so curators know little of how it was furnished or of the floor coverings.

2   Only one photograph of Mere remains in the *Ashton Villa* collection, a family portrait made in 1892 on the occasion of the birth of John McClanahan Jr. An earlier attempt to include her in a multigenerational photo was foiled by Mere herself. In 1889, when Reba Brown (John Stoddart's daughter) became engaged to John McClanahan, Mrs. J. M. Brown hired a photographer to capture the group in the family dining room. But Mere refused to participate and left. In the photo are Mr. and Mrs. J. M. Brown, Bettie, Matilda and Thomas Sweeney, and John Stoddart and Helen Brown, as well as the betrothal couple and several grandchildren.

Mere was very fond of Charles and his wife Estelle, visiting them nearly every day. Rebecca Slack, their daughter, remembers her great-grandmother as "a pioneer woman who faced the unknown West with two small girls and an unbreakable spirit. To her dieing [sic] day she was an individual, independent and self reliant."

3   *Saturday Review*, November 20, 1897 and December 4, 1897.

4   *Ibid.*, January 8, 1898 and April 16, 1898.

5   Transcription of letter dated July 30, 1980 from Rebekah to Nelly (?), in collection of *Ashton Villa*.

6   The date is based on a series of photographs showing Bettie in the costume described later in the text. These portraits were made in New York by A. F. Bradley & Co. According to the New York Historical Society, the studio operated under that name only from 1898 to 1901, then changed to Bradley Studios. The author assumes Bettie did not travel abroad for some time after the Great Storm hit Galveston in September 1900, also discussed later in this chapter.

7   It's not quite clear which royal personage Rebekah (Becky) Brown Allgeyer is referring to in this letter. (July 30, 1980, to Nelly). Franz Josef (1830-1916) was Emperor of Austria-Hungary; his son and heir Rudolph had killed himself, along with his mistress, at Mayerling in 1889. The heir then became Archduke Franz Ferdinand, son of the Emperor's brother Archduke Charles Ludwig. It is not likely that Bettie visited his castle because the Archduke and the Emperor quarreled in 1898 over Ferdinand's choice of a bride; Ferdinand would have been out of favor at the time of Bettie's visit. Probably, then, Mrs. Allgeyer is referring to an imperial residence. The assassination of Franz Ferdinand in 1914 touched off World War I.

8   Probably 6,000 more died on the mainland. Because so many bodies were never found, authorities were never able to agree on a final death figure.

Today visitors to Galveston can view the documentary, "The Great Storm," at the Pier 21 Theater adjacent to the *Elissa* and the Texas Seaport Museum.

9   The Spencer boys' account of the storm is one of the sources of the myth that the Civil War surrender of Galveston took place in *Ashton Villa*. "The surrender of

the city of Galveston to the Union troops was written in her (Mrs. Brown's) house and the table on which it was written is still there." (Paul Lester, *The True Story of the Galveston Flood, As Told by the Survivors*.)

10    Quoted in Suzanne Morris, *The Browns of Ashton Villa*, np.

11    Attempts to bury the bodies at sea failed, for the tide kept returning them to shore. Desperate city officials then ordered the bodies burned.

12    Construction on the first section of the seawall began in the fall of 1902 and was completed two years later; it was subsequently extended to its present length. Grade raising was completed in 1911. Most importantly, the project worked. A hurricane in 1915 of even greater magnitude than the storm of 1900 did little damage to Galveston.

13    The newel posts of the fence were raised but the iron "pickets," or spacers, themselves were not.

14    In his book *Galveston Old and New* (circa 1906), S. B. Southwick wrote this about the 1900 Storm: "The 1900 Hurricane was entirely different from any that have ever come here, or that will probably come again. It would be useless to attempt to describe the Hurricane for it could not be done, and [it] made an impression on people who witnessed it, that will never be effaced. There would have been very little loss of life if precautions had been taken . . . Very little fear was felt, thinking it would be only a repetition of what they had passed through several times. When the horrible situation dawned on them it was too late for action." page 11

# CHAPTER SEVEN

# Riding Around the Pyramids

In the winter of 1901-1902, after the worst damage of the 1900 Storm had been repaired, Bettie began to travel once more. And fortunately for Bettie-afficianados, a journal of part of this trip still exists.

## A SURPRISE MEETING

Not far from *Ashton Villa*, on Tremont Street, lived Colonel William L. Moody (1828-1920), a Virginia-born cotton and banking entrepreneur. He and his wife Pherabe became good friends of the Browns, especially Bettie.

When the Moodys decided to take a trip to Europe and the Mediterranean in 1902, the Colonel kept a journal in the form of letters to the children at home and their families. He and Pherabe, he wrote, were pleasantly surprised on boarding the S.S. *Celtic* in New York on February 8 to be "hailed by a splendid handsome young lady, [with a] queenly air; it was Miss. R. S. [sic] Brown of Galveston."[1] The three traveled about together for much of the trip, the Colonel professing himself very pleased at escorting "the two best looking ladies" on board.

Bettie had begun her trip in typical Bettie fashion. The only passport of hers on record in the National Archives is one she took out for this trip.[2] The application was made in New York just a few days prior to sailing and describes her as 5' 8" tall with blue eyes, regular nose, pointed chin, blond hair and round face. It also clearly states her birth year—in two different places—as 1865 . . . ten years after she was actually born.

This document is also one of the few in which Bettie declared her occupation to be "Artist."

Bettie shared her stateroom on the *Celtic* with at least one other woman, a Mrs. Rew from Chicago who was traveling with her brother-in-law. Moody does not mention a prior relationship between the two, so presumably Bettie was "assigned" Mrs. Rew. The fact that she was not traveling in a private stateroom may indicate that she was trying to hold down expenses, or it may simply be that she was happy for the company.

## MISS B.

The cruise across the Atlantic took about a week and was filled with lounging in deck chairs, enjoying the bounteous meals (ice cream once a day and plenty of salad), making new acquaintances, and attending lectures on the sites that would be visited. Bettie and her "beautiful diamonds" attracted no end of attention in such a setting; it was the Colonel's opinion that she would be "remembered long after the cruise is ended." She endeared herself to him even more on the first day by breaking open a bottle of Park & Tilford's "Old Apple Jack" and sharing a toast with him.

Unfortunately, a bad cold kept Bettie in her cabin for several days . . . not that it seemed to make much difference.

"Sick or well, she is coming to the front," Moody wrote, "her diamonds and queenly air telling even amongst the array of many other rivals." And he noticed also that "Miss B. is growing in admiration of widowers, Mr. Rew one. He is very rich, very stylish, very witty and bright." Rew obliged her with a "very amusing" Valentine on the fourteenth, one of many she received that day. At forty-seven, then, Bettie still attracted the men.

And she and the Moodys continued to get along famously, with Bettie spending much time in their room. "We talk and talk over everything. She and your mother [Pherabe Moody] have talked over all in common." Bettie's new-made friends frequently joined them, sitting until late after dinner and sharing much gaiety and wit.

First stop for the travelers was Funchal, capital of the island of Madeira off the northwest tip of Africa. "At last [we] could see plainly the great Island looming above the sea like a dark blue cloud," Moody wrote, "and in time we could see houses, little white looking spots, and then first trees and then water rushing down the mountains of the island like silver ribbons. . . . I could not convey any idea that would approximate its amazing grandeur and beauty. The sunshine and clouds on its peaks shifted and swapped places."[3]

After exploring the hilly city, the Moodys went back to the ship for the night, but Bettie was one of many passengers who chose to stay on the island in a hotel. The Colonel was quite taken with Funchal's stone-paved streets: "how unlike poor Galveston with its stinking mud holes." Like her friends, Bettie probably explored the Casino, the Catholic cathedral where Christopher Columbus was married, and the beautiful gardens. She also found time to visit at least one shop, for *Ashton Villa* still has a white linen handkerchief embroidered "Madeira" in its collection.

## GIBRALTAR AND BEYOND

By the time the *Celtic* reached Gibraltar for a short stop, Bettie was fully recovered from her cold but disembarked from the ship too late to hire a carriage, as the Moodys did. She returned that evening after visiting the fort and the subterranean galleries inside the Great Rock quite tired "but was made glad finding at her plate a cable from her mother."

Colonel Moody wasn't too pleased with Gibraltar but waxed eloquent about Algiers, on the northern coast of Africa. "The sight, view of the city perhaps was grander, more picturesque and beautiful than any I ever saw before. The buildings dazzlingly white, compact, rising one above the other from the waters until they reached high up on the mountain." Bettie, "gay as a lark," joined the Moodys as they toured the Governor's Winter Palace and traversed the "winding narrow streets."

The next day the trio was joined by a friend of Bettie's as they hired a carriage and guide. "Stopped at shop for Miss B. wanted Mohammedan gown, turban, etc. Wonderful world."[4] Several examples of such attire are still on display in *Ashton Villa*, likely the same ones Bettie bought in Algiers. This is also where she probably bought an enameled copper box filled with sand from the Sahara Desert and still in the house collection, as well as a black coconut coin bank carved with a depiction of the Garden of Eden, which today is in the possession of a Brown descendant. The party visited "stores, mosques, cemeteries and the Lord knows what not," the Colonel grumbled. But he warmed up to dinner at a cafe where they "had two wines and good things to eat."

Upon returning to the ship that evening, they found they were unable to board because of mechanical difficulties. In the confusion, the Moodys lost sight of Bettie as they were forced to travel two miles to New Algiers to get a hotel. Pherabe Moody was "uneasy for her, I not a bit. She can take care of herself anywhere." The Colonel was quite correct; Bettie arrived back at the ship safe and sound.

Disappointment awaited them on Malta (an island just south of Sicily), where rough seas and the Captain's refusal to enter the harbor prevented them from going ashore.

## ATHENS AND TURKEY

From Malta, the *Celtic* sailed east past the Peloponnaise and through the Cyclades Islands to Athens. The Acropolis and the Parthenon awed Colonel Moody, and he, Pherabe, and Bettie visited "lots of old ruins," the Olympic Stadium, Mars Hill "where St. Paul preached," the Museum, and the King's Palace. In between, they took in the shops, too. Bettie bought a "pair [of] shoes, fancy slippers and other worthless things. She has it bad," commented the Colonel, shaking his head.[5]

Bettie apparently stayed over in the city at least one night, because the *Ashton Villa* collection includes a metal souvenir coin from the Hotel de la Grande Bretagne in Athens.

On March first, the *Celtic* reached Constantinople (modern Istanbul) after sailing through the Aegean Sea and the Straits of Dardanelles. Bettie and her friends visited the major sites: the National Museum ("things too old to know of," wrote Colonel Moody), the Mosque of St. Sofia (or Hagia Sophia) built by Constantine, and the Hippodrome. Several items still survive from Bettie's shopping ventures here, among them a pair of small cowhide slippers (marked "First Qualite," of course), a hand mirror of brass and velvet embellished with beads, a small folding book rack, and a Turkish pipe sporting a charm of a crescent moon.

The *Celtic* backtracked a bit from Constantinople, then turned south down the western coast of Turkey to Smyrna (modern Izmir). But Bettie missed Jacob's Well and the travelers' first look at camels there, for she was confined to her cabin once more with a bad cough and cold. The next segment of Colonel Moody's journal is missing, but apparently Bettie had recovered by the time they reached the port of Joppa, jumping off point for Israel, for the *Ashton Villa* collection contains many souvenirs from the Holy Land.

Bettie and the Moodys spent about a week there and visited Bethlehem, Mount Olivet, the Dead Sea, and Jerusalem. This portion of her trip is represented by one of the largest surviving collections of travel items Bettie brought home to Galveston, including a wooden goblet marked from the Dead Sea, a necklace of cloves and beads, a beaded leather belt, and an olive wood cross.

Among the treasures she purchased in Bethlehem were a bridal costume and a photo of a young girl wearing it,[6] a coin necklace, another necklace featuring the crescent moon and star design popular in the Middle East, and a carved wooden rosary, one of many she would bring home from this trip. Perhaps even then, the longtime Episcopalian was giving thought to the conversion that shocked her family years later.

## CLEOPATRA COME HOME

From Joppa, the *Celtic* had but a short sail down the coast to Alexandria, where its Egypt-bound passengers landed to board the train to Cairo. The disembarkation was quite rough, for the seas were high. Guests were let down the side of the ship in a chair attached to ropes, a process that took four hours and left "many seasick, puking and groaning." A four-hour train ride followed, and the weary travelers did not reach Cairo until 11:00 at night.

The Moodys stayed at Shepheard's Hotel, that bastion of European elegance[7]; but Bettie took rooms at the nearby Continental Hotel, which is still standing today and operates as the Continental Savoy. Like Shepheard's, it was located on fashionable Opera Square in the center of town and overlooking the Ezbekiyya Gardens. Pherabe Moody wrote that Shepheard's was the best hotel, but the Continental was "the next best; both fine and beautiful."

And oh, the sights there were to explore in one of the world's oldest cities: the Citadel, the Pyramids of Giza and the enigmatic Sphinx, "black . . . [and] ugly . . . [its] face all battered. . . ."

At Giza the Moodys were treated to another extraordinary sight: their friend Miss Rebecca Ashton Brown, the belle of Galveston, high atop a camel. "She was dressed in many colors," the Colonel wrote home fondly. "The natives I think took her for Cleopatra or [the] Queen of Sheba resurrected."[8] Nearly three decades after portraying the Queen of the Nile in a Mardi Gras parade thousands of miles away, Bettie was at last *really* living the part.

The Moodys left her in Cairo while they went down the Nile. Without the Colonel's journal, it is impossible to know how Bettie occupied her time in the interim. The Egyptian Antiquities Museum had begun construction in 1897 and was completed the year Bettie visited, so she may well have taken in the sights there. Oddly, there are few extant items in the *Ashton Villa* collection traceable to Egypt: a woman's black cotton gauze veil, possibly a marquetry chest of inlaid woods which still stands at the foot of Bettie's bed, and a fly fan with beaded handle to brush away that country's ever-present flies. Certainly she found plenty to do, for Cairo in those days was "very, very gay. Looks like Paris." However, she continued to be plagued with a cough and cold, as many of the Americans were, and joked to Mrs. Moody that she "takes her coffin (coughing) with her."

Late in March, with the Nile travelers returned, the *Celtic* passengers traveled again to Alexandria to reboard their ship. From Egypt, they went to Naples, Italy, where once again the guests split up, some, like the Moodys, remaining in Naples, others going on to Rome. The Colonel's journal notes that Bettie "expected to go from Villefranche to Vienna and return on [the] *Celtic* with us."

## BACK TO EUROPE

That, indeed, was her plan. Bettie ambled from Italy to England, stopping to visit the famous shrine to the Virgin at Lourdes, France (where she bought a pair of souvenir clogs) and the charming mountain town of Mariazell in Austria (where she purchased a mother of pearl and glass trinket box, also on display at *Ashton Villa*). Bettie, who had amassed an enormous amount of silver tableware and flatware over the years, no doubt enjoyed Mariazell's fourteenth-century basilica. For inside, in the Gnadenkapelle, or Chapel of Miracles, a tall silver baldachin covered the church's ancient statue of the Virgin Mary and was flanked by a silver grille given by the Empress Maria Theresa: items large enough to impress even an inveterate collector like Bettie.

From there it was back to old haunts in Vienna and to have her photo made atop the Kahlenberg Heights with "the Bachmayer family."

That she was spending money and enjoying herself is evident from Colonel Moody's comment that, "Billy says deposit was made for Miss Bettie Brown; how much?," intimating that, however much it was, it was probably not enough.[8]

Bettie finished her trip in London before journeying on to Liverpool to sail aboard the SS *Celtic* on April 25. While in England, she may have purchased a pair of cut glass and gilt compotes that still remain in the family and are reputed to have come from "the Royal Stuart castle." Since her brother Charles maintained membership in London's Quator Coronati Lodge,

On her 1902 European trip, Bettie (at left) visited the Kahlenberg Heights in Vienna with the Bachmayer family. (Courtesy *Ashton Villa*)

Bettie likely had a wide circle of acquaintances to call upon while there.

Thus ended Bettie's 1902 trip abroad.[10] The trip was undoubtedly much like those she'd taken before; the difference lies in its remarkable documentation through the pen of two friends and traveling companions.

## Notes: Chapter Seven

1  All quotations in this chapter, unless otherwise noted, are from Colonel Moody's journal in the collection of the Moody Mansion and Museum, Galveston, Texas. February 8, 1902.

2  Prior to World War I, U. S. citizens were not required to have passports while traveling abroad, though many did. Bettie lied about her age on another occasion, as well. The 1900 Census for Galveston County quite clearly shows the birth year and age of everyone in the household—except for Bettie. In her case, both numbers are deliberately illegible.

3  February 16, 1902.

4  "Wonderful world" was Colonel Moody's trademark saying. February 21-23, 1902.

5  February 26-27, 1902.

6  This is the same costume Bettie lent to Mary Moody for a "peasant dance" during her 1911 debut year events. Mary described it as "a red satin skirt with over garment of red, blue, green and yellow striped material coarsely woven . . . worn [with] a silk sash to correspond. A red woolen [sic] coat beautifully embroidered in the same colors with cap trimmed with coins and beads and also a necklace of coins and beads completed the costume." (From Diary of Mary Moody [Northen], page 35, in collection of Moody Mansion and Museum, Galveston.)

7  There is still a Shepheard's Hotel in Cairo, but the original Victorian structure which stood near Opera Square was destroyed in the 1952 revolution.

8  March 13, 1902.

9  Bettie apparently had accounts at Moody National Bank; "Billy" was probably the Colonel's son, W. L. Moody Jr.

10  The itinerary Bettie and the Moodys followed was a popular one. The Hamburg-America Line also adver-

tised in the *Galveston Daily News* its winter cruises "to the Orient" aboard the *Auguste Victoria* that traveled much the same route: Madeira, Gibraltar, Spain, Italy, Morocco, Turkey, Greece, and Egypt.

CHAPTER EIGHT

# Troubled Times

The 1902 trip to Europe was not Bettie's last venture overseas, but it was fortunate that the cruise proved such a pleasant one as more troubled times lay ahead.

## DEATHS IN THE FAMILY

About a year after Bettie's return from the *Celtic* voyage, the family matriarch died at the age of ninety-seven. "Mere," Mrs. Brown's mother who had braved the rigors of a young Texas with two small daughters, died in 1903 in her own bed on the third floor of *Ashton Villa*. Sarah Warner Moses Stoddart Rhodes was fondly remembered by her family as always wearing "her widow's bonnet, long black veiling hanging down the back, little question mark curls on her forehead. Her smile was her trademark."

Estelle Austin Brown, Charles' wife and a favorite of the Brown family, died less than two weeks after giving birth to the couple's seventh child, Estelle Rose, on April 15, 1905. Not long after, Charles married Elizabeth Hunt, a woman cordially disliked by his family and, soon, by Charles himself. Seldom invited to *Ashton Villa*, Elizabeth retaliated by christening her

Dickinson home (in the mainland section of Galveston County) *Brown Villa*.

Two years after her own mother's death, Rebecca Ashton Stoddart Brown began to fail. She suffered from heart problems but managed to stay fairly active until just a few months before her death on October 5, 1907 at the age of seventy-six.[1] She was buried in the Episcopal Cemetery next to her husband, James Moreau Brown, and with her mother and stepfather. The *Galveston Daily News* eulogized her as "one of the pioneer women of Galveston" and declared that "the (Brown) family is one of the oldest and most prominently connected with the history of Galveston of any in the city."

Rebecca's will had been written in 1898 and left *Ashton Villa*—"my House Ground(s) Stable Horses and Carriages Silver everything in the House"—to Bettie. Aside from a few other specific bequests, the five Brown children were to equally divide the remainder of her estate, consisting of leases, stocks, bonds, real estate, and cash: a total of nearly $120,000 (excluding the $18,000 value of *Ashton Villa*).[2]

Since James Brown had refused to have any court involvement in his estate beyond the proving and recording of his will, there is no inventory from his 1895 probate to compare with his wife's. And the exact amount of the fortune he bequeathed Rebecca is unknown. But that her estate was substantially less than what he had left the family, just twelve years earlier, can be inferred from an astonishing item in Mrs. Brown's inventory.

Listed among the assets of her estate were claims against her oldest child, John Stoddart Brown, personally for $71,175 and against the J. S. Brown Hardware Company he managed for an additional $71,713.32—more than $142,000 altogether—which was described in the inventory as the value of securities belonging to her estate and entrusted to John's care by Rebecca in her lifetime. That amount added to the rest would have made her total estate more than a quarter of a million dollars, still substantially less than what the family believed their father James had accumulated, but far from a paltry figure.

## A THORNY PROBLEM

It seemed that on January 1, 1896, just after James Brown's death, Rebecca had given a complete and unconditional power of attorney to her eldest son John "to attend to all my business and property of all kinds, to receive and collect all money or property due or to become due to me . . . to hold for me all my Stocks, Bonds[,] notes, real Estate and other property of all Kinds[,] to invest or change investments[,] to sell and convey by Deed . . . any of my property real[,] personal or mixed."[3] This was to save the widow "the worry, trouble and annoyance of any and all business matters" and was done in the presence of both Bettie and "J. M. Brown" (probably Moreau's son, J. M. Brown II, then eighteen years old).

John was the oldest of the Brown children, so it may have been natural for his mother to turn to him. But it is revealing of Rebecca Brown's attitude that she entrusted the job to him—a man—and not to Bettie, who not only lived at *Ashton Villa* with her, close to hand, but had been judged by her father, who "rarely made a mistake in selecting his lieutenants," as perfectly capable of understanding business affairs.

Over the ensuing years until her death, John executed leases in the several commercial structures Rebecca Brown owned, released liens against notes properly paid, and helped her file at least one suit.[4] When his daughter Reba's husband died suddenly, John also served as executor of his estate (1897).

The Galveston County deed records are filled with John's real estate dealings, most of them undertaken with his wife Helen. He bought acreage on Dickinson Bayou at a sheriff's

117

sale, then resold it. Through the hardware store, he bought land in what was then the outskirts of Galveston, on Avenue P 1/2 (today a residential area a few blocks from the *1839 Williams Home*). He sold lots adjoining his own home on Broadway, property his father had given him in 1876, then sold the note against it. And in the 1905 City Directory, John listed himself as president of the Galveston Land, Oil & Gas Company, through which he apparently sold real estate and owned part of the Dickinson Oil Company.[5]

Most of all, John Stoddart Brown filed a lot of lawsuits.

Just one index to Galveston County court records lists twenty-four cases filed by John through J. S. Brown Hardware Company.[6] Some he won, but others cost John money. Late in 1905, for example, he had won a judgment against James A. and H. L. Ewing of Jefferson County. To recover his award, John caused an execution to be levied upon certain property the Ewings had sold to the First Christian Church of Beaumont. Naturally, the church filed an injunction to stop the sale and won because they had been innocent purchasers. The hardware store had to pay the costs of that suit and, in the end, only recovered about 9 percent of the original judgment. In the meantime, the entire process had dragged on for eight years, costing court and attorney time. In another suit, J. S. Brown Hardware versus K. H. Cawthon, eighteen years passed from the initial filing until the recovery of the $256 award plus interest and court costs, a minimal return for the time involved.

To fund all these dealings, John, according to his siblings, had been using his mother's stocks to secure his notes. He was also using them to shore up the hardware store, which was failing; he even owed his mother close to $20,000 in rent. The inventory for Rebecca Brown's estate indicates that by the time she died, John had already been forced by his creditors to sell assets such as San Antonio City sewer bonds.

The gist of the matter was, as Moreau explained it to his son, "it now appears that we [the five children] shall each receive about $5,000 instead of the $100,000 we anticipated. . . ."[7] His statement indicates that the children of J. M. Brown believed his estate to be worth about half a million dollars. Instead, it had been reduced by about 70 percent.[8]

The Browns of *Ashton Villa* were no longer as wealthy as they had once been.

## GOING TO COURT

Charles, Moreau, Bettie, and Matilda filed suit against John to recover the monies, but the case never came to court. In an apparent acknowledgement that one "can't get blood from a turnip," they settled out of court with John and his wife, Helen, in November and December of 1908, a year after their mother's death.[9]

John and Helen had been using his one-fifth interest in Rebecca's real estate holdings as collateral, a move which must have infuriated the others. Now, in return for his conveying them that interest, Charles, Moreau, Bettie, and Matilda sold John and Helen their share of Lot 2, Block 622 (property fronting on The Strand between 22nd and 23rd streets).[10]

They also filed a separate document releasing "the said John S. Brown from all further claim or claims against him of every kind and nature whatsoever, both as Executors [of Mrs. Brown's estate] and [as] individuals." As compensation for their dropping the suit, John conveyed to his brothers and sisters his claim to J. S. Brown Hardware Company.[11] A few weeks later, the last document was filed when John gave up his claim to Rebecca's stocks, bonds, and monies (including what he'd given Helen) as part of the "settlement of all matters of every kind between us . . . such settlement embracing all matters, personaly [sic] and individual [sic], as well as Executors of the estate of Mrs. Rebecca A. Brown, deceased. . . ."[12]

So bitter were the feelings between John, Bettie, Matilda, and Moreau that when John died in 1912, his obituary listed only his brother Charles. The other siblings refused to attend his funeral.[13] What makes their discord even sadder is that friends of John's praised him as generous to a fault, always giving money to those in need.

Early in 1909, with Charles in place as president of the company, the bankrupt J. S. Brown Hardware Company was placed in the hands of a trustee who was to sell everything it owned to pay off debts: stocks of merchandise, store furniture, claims and notes owed the business, and lands.[14]

Thus the business established by James Moreau Brown decades earlier, and once the largest of its kind in the western United States, came to an end.

## Notes: Chapter Eight

1   Rebecca Brown's death, at *Ashton Villa*, was due to "cardiac insufficiency," probably congestive heart failure. (Mortuary Report, Galveston Health Department, Book 5, January 1, 1904 to January 31, 1910.)

2   Rebecca Brown's estate included shares of stock in American Manufacturing Company of West Virginia, Galveston Wharf Company (of which James Brown had been president), Galveston Gas Company (of which James had been vice president), Southern Cotton Press & Manufacturing Company, The Savings & Loan Company, and the First National Bank of Rusk, Texas. Among her real estate holdings, most of them deeded to her by her husband in 1893 as her separate property, were choice lots in the wharf area, downtown, and behind *Ashton Villa*. (Will: Book 52, pages 516-522. Inventory: Book 52, page 610. Galveston County, Texas Probate Records)

Her will specified that Matilda would receive her diamond ring and breast pin, as well as the diamond earrings she had bequeathed to Estelle Brown (Charles' wife), who had predeceased her. In addition, Bettie was to select an "air Lume" (heirloom) for each child, grandchild, and daughter-in-law.

3   Galveston County Deed Book 136, pages 133-134.

4   Galveston County District Court, Case #17955, Rebecca Ashton Brown versus A. H. Pierce, guardians of the estate of Menard James. The two parties each owned undivided halves of Lot 10, Block 685 in downtown Galveston; the suit was filed to divide the property or sell it if it was incapable of being divided. The court eventually ruled for sale, and the lot was purchased by George Sealy for $6,655. (That block is now the location of The Railroad Museum.)

The author also found listings of two other suits filed by or against Rebecca Brown in the period 1898-1909 but no records.

5    John acquired his interest in Dickinson Oil as the result of a lawsuit the hardware store filed against Fred McC. Nichols and the company, which was settled in 1901. Nichols transferred nearly $3,000 worth of his shares of stock to J. S. Brown Hardware Company. Galveston County Deed Book 186, page 32.

6    Index to General Docket No. 6. Unfortunately, the records of all these cases have been transferred to storage in Houston, and the author was unable to research them.

7    Letter dated October 7, 1981 from J. Moreau Brown III to Judy Schiebel and quoting letter from Dr. Moreau R. Brown to J. Moreau Brown II; in collection of *Ashton Villa.*

8    Though Moreau and Charles were successful in their respective careers, and Bettie showed evidence of the ability to have done equally well if she'd had the chance, none of James Brown's children came close to equalling him in the acquisition of wealth.

9    Helen became involved in the process because John, foreseeing what would happen, had transferred to her "for her better support and maintenance" all his interest in his mother's estate on March 25, 1908. Galveston County Deed Book 226, pages 435-436.

10    Galveston County Deed Book 231, pages 344-345. John and Helen eventually were forced to mortgage this property to pay a note they owed to Security Investment Company.

The property owned by Rebecca Brown's estate was: Lot 14 in Block 682 (location of J. S. Brown Hardware Company on The Strand), Lot 2 in Block 622 (which the siblings gave John), the south 1/3 of Lots 6 and 7 in Block 503 (fronting on the alley between Market and

Postoffice streets, between 23rd and 24th streets), Lots 1 and 2 in Block 503 (which fronted onto Market Street near 24th Street), Lots 8 and 9 in Block 264 (on Sealy Avenue near *Ashton Villa*), Lots 1, 2 and 3 in the southwest Block of Outlot 157 (fronting on Avenue T between 43rd and 45th streets), 6 acres in the north end of Lot 73 in Section 1 of Galveston Island, and 1,382 acres in Bellews League in Harris County. This last property was then 9 to 12 miles from Houston on Buffalo Bayou and had been purchased by J. M. Brown. The 1910 tax rolls for Galveston County list the value of these properties—excluding *Ashton Villa*—at nearly $75,000, on which the estate paid $874.54 in taxes. Bettie personally paid an additional $252.57 in state, school, county, and special taxes on the house and its four lots, which the county had valued at $21,650.

11  Galveston County Deed Book 231, pages 350-351.

12  Galveston County Deed Book 231, page 346.

13  John Stoddart Brown died April 23, 1912 at the age of sixty-four at John Sealy Hospital "after an illness of several weeks, the end being not unexpected by relatives and close friends." Helen de Lespine Brown had died in 1910. John was survived by his three daughters: Reba McClanahan Gaines (Mrs. William), Helen Henderson (Mrs. George, the first of her three husbands), and Edgene Tipps (Mrs. Eugene).

14  Galveston County Deed Book 232, pages 368-369.

# Lady of Charity

By the time the suit with John was settled, the makeup of *Ashton Villa* had changed again. Matilda's son Charles James Sweeney, "C. J.," a construction foreman, had married in 1907 and brought his New York-born bride, Guinevere Graham, to live in the big brick mansion on Broadway. Their son Charles J. Jr. was born a year later. C. J.'s older brother Moreau, unmarried and a freight broker specializing in cotton, also lived at *Ashton Villa*.[1] But Alice, the youngest Sweeney, was off in a Peekskill, New York boarding school most of the year.

## THE LONG WAY TO SCHOOL

In July 1906, Alice's grandmother Rebecca, mother Matilda, and Aunt Bettie had accompanied her to St. Gabriel's School for her freshman year. The first stop was a family vacation in Atlantic City, New Jersey, where the four ladies met Dr. Moreau Brown, his wife Louise, son J. M., and daughter Becky at the Rudolf Hotel. Atlantic City was a very popular resort with a number of fashionable hotels, a boardwalk suitable for promenades, and plenty of amusements for everyone.

Bettie, her nephew Moreau, and niece Rebekah visited Atlantic City, New Jersey in 1906. Here they pose in a wicker "Boardwalk chair," used to promenade along the seashore. (Courtesy *Ashton Villa*)

This is the occasion that caused the change in the spelling of Rebekah Brown Allgeyer's name, who had been christened Rebecca Alice Brown when she was born in 1895. But mayhem resulted when the eleven-year-old picked up the family mail at the front desk and innocently opened a note addressed to "Miss Rebecca A. Brown"—her name, of course, but also that of her Aunt Bettie. The note proved to be a rather warm love letter from one of Bettie's admirers. To prevent such an embarrassment happening again, Rebecca became Rebekah.[2]

By mid-August, Matilda had returned to Galveston and Alice was in school, so Bettie and her mother moved on to the Mizzen Top Hotel in Pawling, New York, just a few miles from the Connecticut line and not far from Orange County where James Brown was born. "Quiet and cool," the hotel sat atop a series of rolling hills—which offered a "panoramic view from the Golf Links"—and was a vast, Second-Empire-style frame building with a long front veranda. It was also, according to Bettie, "full of old people."

The pair returned to Galveston, but October found Bettie and Matilda once again headed north to visit Alice. With a still-single C. J. in tow, they visited Albany, New York and nearby Troy, staying at the Rensselaer Hotel. (Matilda noted politely that the service was "not New York.") Since C. J. married a New York girl in Atlantic City the following year, he may have met her on this trip.

## A CHANGE OF PHILOSOPHY

Mrs. Brown joked that their visit to Mizzen Top, with all its elderly guests, was research for Bettie, who had developed a new passion—philanthropy.

What changed Bettie's focus is not clear. She had been involved in her father's charities for many years before his death, but few in her own right. Perhaps discovering the years of abuse Matilda endured began to awaken her to the plight of so many women and children in Victorian America's legal structure, which generally favored the husband. Certainly the horror of the 1900 Storm would have fully opened her eyes to the needs of those around her and left her with a more sober outlook toward life. Whatever the cause—or causes—Bettie clearly undertook a change in lifestyle following the Storm.

She did not give up her beloved traveling, as witness her 1902 cruise and several more she would yet take. But she did curtail her trips, remaining in Galveston for months at a time and in seasons when she had previously fled north. Nor did she lose her love for beautiful clothes and jewelry; but photographs of her from the early 1900s on show her in general more sedately dressed and wearing less finery.

Even her expression seems to have altered in these later photos. Where she had once gazed at the camera forthrightly, even a bit cocky, now she seems more subdued, sometimes to the point of melancholy.[3]

## THE LETITIA ROSENBERG HOME

Her first choice for a philanthropy was probably directly due to her mother's influence, for Rebecca Brown had been a benefactor of the Letitia Rosenberg Home for Women since its inception in 1888.

Organized by Galveston women and housed for many years in a rented structure, the Home cared for indigent and elderly women from Galveston and throughout the region, its somewhat depressing motto being "Within our Gray Walls Mothers, Widows, and Sisters Dwell."[4] An all-male board of directors made many of the financial decisions, but the daily operations of the Home were supervised by the Board of Lady Managers. In 1896 the Home moved into a spacious new structure on 25th Street (or Rosenberg) that was built with a $30,000 bequest from Galveston entrepreneur Henry Rosenberg (1824-1893).

Exactly when Bettie became a member of the Board of Lady Managers is unclear; a resolution passed after her death reports she was elected in March 1902. But the minute book which ends April 23 does not list her, and there is a subsequent gap in the records until 1905. Likely she was tapped sometime later in 1902 after her return from Europe to fill a vacancy on the twenty-five-member board.

Within two years, Bettie had become president of the board, a position she would hold until early in 1918. And in that period, she gave of herself unstintingly to the Home.

## MADAME PRESIDENT

Bettie's first concern was to build up the Home's precarious finances. She deposited most monetary gifts into the Reserve Fund, rather than using them for daily expenses as had been the case before. By 1906 she had convinced the board to amend the by-laws and place that fund under the president's control, and it grew steadily under her care.

Madame President kept a tight rein on expenses. So small a matter as the amount of money to be spent on flowers for funerals passed her review. The ladies were persuaded that "the sending of an unpretentious memento would convey the sympathy of the members of the board with equal effect as an expensive one, and that considering the charitable purposes of this organization the money saved could be used to better purpose."[5] Later, Bettie thriftily purchased a dozen tablespoons "with Octagon soap wrappers."

When stock owned by the Home was to be sold, Bettie dealt with the matter, and her handling was always "greatly to the satisfaction of the board." As president, she also presided over the annual joint meetings of the board of directors and the Board of Lady Managers, to the praise of all.

Special events such as the Flower Ball (in which niece Alice Sweeney portrayed a daisy), the Charity Ball, and the Baby Show were major fundraisers for the Home. When one of these or other, smaller events failed to raise the anticipated amount, Bettie always had an alternative to make up the difference: providing the supper for the Artillery Club Ball, for example, with proceeds going to the Home. And she had an additional and highly unique method—selling her Angora kittens for $5 and donating the money.[6] She regularly opened *Ashton Villa* for "silver teas" to raise money for the Home much as Rebecca Brown had done for church benefits such as the Ladies Aid Society.

Bettie also personally gave small to moderate sums of money from time to time and for specific purposes: underwriting the expenses of one of the Home's "inmates," as the women were called, to visit Longview, paying the gardener to set out palm trees and other plants, buying an oil stove for the kitchen and shoes and spectacles for the residents.

Upon her return from the Atlantic City and New York trip in 1906, she held the biweekly board meeting at *Ashton Villa* and treated the ladies to "an elaborate breakfast . . . This delightful opportunity to meet Miss Brown socially after her two months absence from the city was greatly enjoyed by all present not only because of the gracious hospitality, but because the board was heartily glad to welcome her back into their midst, as in her absence she had been greatly missed."[7]

## A BUSY SCHEDULE

As indeed she had.

Few days passed without Bettie traveling the four or five blocks between *Ashton Villa* and the Home. It was the president's "privilege" to see to selling the dilapidated windmill, supervise the construction of a new cistern, shop for the best prices of items needed for the Home, buy and sell the cows that provided milk, pay bank notes and repair bills, and report and deposit all monies received. When the need for an electric light on the front steps caught her eye, she paid for the project by selling two cats. Even the customary beer given to the construction workers laboring on the addition was donated by Bettie.

She was zealous in attending meetings and missed only a few. She was absent, however, for nearly three months in the early fall of 1907 during her mother's final illness and death.[8] The board secretary diligently recorded her trip to Mexico[9] in September 1910 and to Italy in the winter of 1911-1912, probably her last trip abroad. Other than those excursions, the former globe-trotter stayed close to home.

In 1908, with the high cost of physically raising the Home and its grounds (part of the city-wide project after the 1900 Storm), Bettie decided the financial situation was critical enough to warrant a bold step: going to the County of Galveston for money. She wrote to Alexander Gomez, County Commissioner and Chair of Charity Finances, and gave him a quick history of the Home, reminding him that, prior to the Storm, the county had supported it. "Since then we have worked and struggled," Bettie wrote, "to care for these dear little old Women who's [sic] feet are set in the path of lifes [sic] descending sun, unaided by the County . . . Will you in your good heart show charity and recommend your Committee to set aside, for this institution $35.00 per month to assist in caring for these Women[,] this City's poor."[10]

Bettie followed up her letter to Gomez with a personal visit to answer his questions, "which were many. . . . Miss Brown also saw every County Commissioner (except Mr. Dick) and the Judge."[11] Her efforts were successful, and the Lady Managers' request was granted thanks to "Miss Brown's untiring efforts in behalf of the Home."

## THE TANGO BALL

While most people approved of Bettie's direction of the Home, she did meet some serious opposition in 1913 when she suggested that the annual fundraising dance be a Tango Ball at the Hotel Galvez, built on the beachfront two years earlier.

The City Ministerial Association protested *vigorously* and denounced the new-fangled tango, somewhat akin to the flamenco and thought by many to be scandalously lewd, as "both improper and absolutely harmful to the morals of the community." To which Miss Rebecca Ashton Brown, president of the Board of Lady Managers, replied: "I think it an outrage. It is making a mountain out of a molehill. The tango dance, when properly executed, is perfectly harmless. Because a man may now and then take a drink of wine, does that make him a drunkard?"[12]

Mrs. Harris Kempner, chairwoman of the Ball and no lightweight in Galveston social circles herself, proved equally intractable and refused to cancel or change the Ball. So the clergy, "having in view the best religious and moral interests of the city," issued a formal protest and maintained that their feelings about this lewdness were shared by the Elks, Kaiser Wilhelm of Germany, the Woodmen of the World, and—the clincher—the authorities of the University of Texas. The Ministerial Association then shared its opinion that people would give cheerfully "as soon as the actual needs of the institution were set before them."[13]

One can only wonder what Bettie said about this naive view of fundraising.

Thanks to Galveston's ministers, the Tango Ball enjoyed a "larger than expected attendance," including several score of army officers stationed at Fort Crockett. Miss Rebecca Ashton Brown and the other Lady Managers formed the receiving line that night and happily deposited nearly $700 for their efforts.

## HELPING THE CHILDREN

Bettie's second main charity during this period was the Home for Homeless Children, founded in 1894 as the Society for Friendless Children. The 1900 Storm destroyed the building and killed many of the children in residence; the city and county of Galveston then helped the group purchase a house at 1019 16th Street.[14] The Home was unique for its day in that it accepted not orphans, but children who needed shelter because of parental illness or abuse.

Unfortunately, the minute books for 1904-1905 and 1906-1907 are missing, so it is not clear when Bettie was elected to that board. She does appear as a member in the 1908 minutes. As with the Letitia Rosenberg Home, there were two boards. Nine women composed the board of directors and twelve men formed an advisory board; on it were such Galveston luminaries as Rabbi Henry Cohen, John Sealy, and Aaron Blum.

The extent of Bettie's involvement with the Home for Homeless Children is hard to gauge. She did not serve as an officer, and the minutes usually refer to positions (*i.e.*, the Investigating Committee) rather than names, so it's difficult for the researcher to pick her out. Bettie was placed in charge of the collection boxes located around town for donations and periodically handed in that money.[15] The boxes would prove a major task, as she had to physically go to every place each month to collect the money, and the boxes were the frequent target of petty thieves.

From time to time, Bettie also offered to find a dentist to work on the children's teeth free of charge or served on the committee to find a new location for the Home. ("Negroes" had bought the adjacent property and opened a "pleasure resort" where they served liquor; the Lady Managers were concerned.) On meeting the children downtown one afternoon after their visit to "the Picture Show," she took them to Schott's ice cream parlour for a treat of ice cream and soda. But Mr. Schott, she reported to the board, donated the refreshments himself.[16]

## TAG DAY

In the few years she worked with the Children's Home, Bettie's biggest task was to chair "Tag Day," a joint fundraising effort between the Home and the Johanna Runge Free Kindergarten. The minutes are rather vague about just how the event worked; it appears that the volunteers fanned out across Galveston and "sold" tags commemorating the day.[17]

From the date of the initial meeting at the Rosenberg Library, Bettie was the overwhelming choice as chairwoman because of the quality of her work with the Women's Home. "Mrs. William Stewart, president of the Home for Homeless Children board of directors, in appointing Miss Rebecca Ashton Brown executive chairman made the initial step to success, as Miss Brown's executive ability is well known. There is no half-hearted work about what this lady does. When she goes into anything time is put at a discount. Enterprise and energy have no leisure to hear what might happen, as all is centered on what will happen if good work is done. Hence the success this chairman always achieves in what she sets her heart and mind to do."[18]

Bettie did not seek such compliments. Quite the opposite, in fact. She preferred to keep quiet about her volunteer work unless the lure of her name would aid the cause, much as her father had done. Christopher Byrne, bishop of the Catholic Church, later told a reporter that "her charities were of the gospel kind(;) she did not let her 'right hand know what her left hand did.'"[19]

But by 1911, after three years on the Tag Day committee, Bettie stopped attending board meetings at the Children's Home. She had already missed a number of meetings in 1909, and in 1910 she attended only two from June through the end of the year, though she had served once again as chairman of Tag Day in the spring. At one of her last board meetings, Bettie "asked to be relieved of the labor of collecting the money from the boxes as her time is so much occupied at home."[20] This may refer to additional responsibilities that fell on her in the wake of the hardware store's bankruptcy and other financial troubles, or simply to the time she was spending helping Matilda with daughter Alice's debut.

Her name continued to be listed on the Home's board even in 1912 but was penciled through and a new name added, indicating that she had been replaced.

Clearly, when she had a choice of where to spend her volunteer time and energies, she chose the Rosenberg Home, as she continued to be quite active as its president during this period despite being "so much occupied at home."

## FAILING HEALTH

She remained president of the Rosenberg board until February 1918, but long before that date the minutes show indications of some health problem.

Bettie meticulously signed each minute entry as approved by her. Her signature was large and flowing, sweeping with curlicues in the capital letters as she wrote "Rebecca Ashton Brown."

But by the end of 1911 her signature had become wobbly, as if she were having difficulty holding the pen. It then improved for a while, worsening again perceptibly in the fall of 1913 when it became almost illegible. Within a year, she had shortened it from her customary "Rebecca Ashton Brown" to simply "R A Brown." One can almost trace the ups and downs of her health from the legibility of her handwriting. By mid-1917 the minutes record many meetings she attended, but the entries are either not signed at all or are signed for her by secretary Esther Neethe.

On February 8, 1918, Bettie attended the regular meeting of the Board of Lady Managers accompanied by the president of the board of directors. On her behalf, he tendered her resignation which had become "necessary in the interest of her health." Shortly thereafter, the board of directors took charge of the Home's investments, which Bettie had overseen, and changed banks. Were they trying to prevent her regaining control? More likely, the board was saying it trusted no one else as it had Bettie, to whom the men had relinquished much control.

At its next meeting, the Lady Managers named her honorary president for life and officially expressed their appreciation of Bettie's work. "Resolved further, that in severing her official connection with the Home the board desires to convey its keen appreciation of her long and splendid service to the Home, which has been given unreservedly through good times and bad. To her untiring energy and conscientious care for the interests of the institution is due in a large measure its present condition of prosperity and efficiency. She always brought to the discharge of her duties as president of the Home that zeal and fidelity which has characterized her every work. No trouble was too great for her to take, no detail too small to escape her attention in all matters affecting the welfare of the Home. In her resignation the institution loses the most valuable and faithful officer in its history wherein is forever written the results of years of consistent effort and which will always stand as a monument."[21]

James Moreau Brown would have been proud of his daughter.

## Notes: Chapter Nine

1    Within a few years, Moreau went into partnership with Will E. Sorrells and a third agent located in Dallas, Texas to establish Sorrells & Sweeney, freight brokers and forwarding agents. Brother C. J. worked for them as a clerk for a time, then went out on his own with Sweeney's Sporting Goods Store at 308 22nd Street. While Moreau lived at *Ashton Villa* until his untimely death from tuberculosis in 1918, C. J. and Guinevere had moved out by 1913. (1913 and 1916 Galveston City Directory)

2    This was not Becky's last brush with one of her aunts. The following New Year, she appeared for dinner at *Ashton Villa* in a yellow dress "with a real lace rose point lace bertha off the shoulders." But Aunt Matilda ordered her to change into a more decent dress. Matilda also refused to leave her anything in her will after Becky left one Thanksgiving dinner early to attend horse races: "Rebekah went to the races," she wrote above the marked-out bequest.

3    A notable exception is the series of portraits showing Bettie in her famous lace coat.

4    Candidates had to apply for admission, be recommended by a board member, and pass a strict medical exam. Much like modern retirement homes, those who had the means were expected to leave some large sum of money, between $500 and $800, to the Home after their death. Rarely, the Lady Managers allowed temporary boarders.

5    Minute Book of the Board of Lady Managers of the Letitia Rosenberg Home, hereinafter referred to as L. R. Minute Book: October 13, 1905.

6    Bettie paid the plumber $4.85 to pump water out of the basement, the money "being part of five dollars ($5.00) realized from the Sale of one Persian cat." (L. R. Minute Book, February 23, 1906.) Several other similar entries

may be found. Thus the records confirm a longstanding family legend.

7   L. R. Minute Book October 18, 1906.

8   Rebecca Brown bequeathed a chandelier for the Home's front hall, which was hung early in 1909.

9   Traveling to Mexico from Galveston was as easy in Bettie's day as going to Europe. The *Daily News* regularly carried advertisements for steamship companies that sailed from either Galveston or nearby Texas City to several Mexican ports, where passengers could connect with the Mexican National Railway system to their final inland destination.

10  Letter dated September 19, 1908 and pasted into frontispiece of 1907-1911 Minute Book.

11  Galveston County was governed then, as it is now, by a commissioner's court which is headed by the county judge, an administrative rather than a judicial position.

12  *Galveston Daily News*, December 29, 1984.

13  Petition dated November 18, 1913, in the collection of the Galveston-Texas History Center at the Rosenberg Library.

14  In 1912, after Bettie resigned from the board, Morris Lasker donated $15,000 to repair and furnish the building which was renamed the Lasker Home in his honor. Today it is part of the Children's Crisis Center, which maintains the records of the Home.

15  One night in 1909, burglars broke into *Ashton Villa* while the family slept and made off with some jewelry, loose cash, and "a money box belonging to the Home for Homeless Children." No one heard anything because the whole family had spent the day decorating the carriage Alice would drive in the next day's carnival parade, and all were tired out. Their efforts worked, however: Alice's tallyho won first prize for best decorated vehicle.

Page from Alice Sweeney scrapbook, dated August 6, 1909.

16  Minutes of the Home for Homeless Children: March 10 and March 17, 1908; March 3 and April 14, 1908; September 22, 1908.

17  The first Tag Day in 1908 was a roaring success and raised $2,000 to be split between the two organizations.

18  *Galveston Daily News*, April 7, 1908, page 10.

19  Charlotte Reid Seybold, "Resort Attracted Texas Beauty," September 18, 1953.

James M. Brown's obituary states: "He never turned his back on the needy. His private charities will never be known. It is said that he contributed at one time $5,000 for the relief of the distressed after the great fire in Galveston (*i.e.*, 1885), but at the time nothing was known about it, and perhaps this is the first time his contribution has seen the light of public print. Many families will miss his gifts this Christmas, and many will drop a silent tear when they learn that their erstwhile benefactor is no more. His contributions to charity, it is said, are known only to his youngest [*sic*] daughter, Miss Bettie. . . ."

20  Home for Homeless Children Board Minutes, May 31, 1910.

21  L. R. Minute Book, February 22, 1918.

# The Prime of Miss Alice

The years from about 1909 through the mid-teens were happy ones for Bettie. Though she may have begun suffering from some health problems, she was busy with her volunteer work and an occasional trip, and *Ashton Villa* was once more the site of a beautiful young woman making her debut.

## ALICE SWEENEY

Matilda's youngest child, Matilda Alice Sweeney, was born in the Sweeney home on Avenue L but grew up in *Ashton Villa* after her parents' divorce in 1896. She had weathered the 1900 Storm within the mansion's red brick walls and watched the family's internal dissension after Mrs. Brown's death through the eyes of a teenager. Now Alice Sweeney was ready to make her mark in the world.

Alice debuted in polite Galveston society in the winter of 1909-1910. And her mother and aunt were determined to "send off" this tall, lovely young woman in old-fashioned Brown style.

On February 2, 1910, they entertained over 400 women at an *Ashton Villa* reception acclaimed as "one of the hand-

somest events of the season." The house was filled with flowers: large pink Killarney roses in the Gold Room, white hya-
cinths and pink azaleas in the front hall, red carnations in
Bettie's silver baskets on the coffee table, more roses mixed
with violets in the family dining room with its crimson shades,
and baskets of red and white roses on the dining room table.
Matilda wore black, C. J.'s wife Guinevere was in light blue
satin, and Alice was a proper debutante in pink satin and lace.
But her Aunt Bettie, who would turn fifty-six in only a few days,
"graced her drawing room with queenly dignity," attired in "a
white val lace robe en train"—her favorite style.

A bevy of Galveston's most prominent matrons and debu-
tantes formed the house party. And the reception which was
supposed to have lasted only from four to seven was so popular
that the party did not break up until after midnight, as husbands, beaus, and even "the young gentlemen on their way to
the Quartet Society rehearsal," all made their way to *Ashton
Villa*.[1]

Bettie accompanied her niece to many of Galveston's elite
social events over the next few years. At the Artillery Ball, the
highlight of the Christmas season, Alice wore yellow satin and
blue chiffon while Bettie wowed the guests with a "Parisian
gown of pompadour chiffon" over duchess satin. Alice made
the Grand March that night on the arms of Artillery Club vice
president Bartlett O. Moore; older brother Moreau also
attended as Club secretary.

By 1911-1912, the winter of the debut of Miss Mary
Moody (Colonel Moody's granddaughter and daughter of W. L.
Jr.), Alice was in a position, being officially "out," to entertain
her friend. And again Mama and Aunt Bettie and Guinevere
Sweeney (assisted by C. J. Jr., "without whom no gathering at
*Ashton Villa* would be complete") put all the resources of the
house at her disposal. Alice hosted a bridge party for Mary and
two other girls; one of its highlights proved to be, not bridge

and cake, but viewing the "various art collections of Rebecca Ashton Brown, from headgear to laces and curios of all nations. . . ."[2] Despite the financial problems that beset the Browns, Bettie and Matilda made sure Alice was not embarrassed by a poor showing. The food was lavish and the prizes genteel: a silver compote, a crystal and silver bonbonniere, and a silver and crystal puff box, among them.[3] Even Miss Moody, raised in wealth, could not cavil at *Ashton Villa* hospitality: "Little need be said of this party, as everyone knows that all given in this beautiful home are always most charming affairs and I indeed feel fortunate in having been included as an honoree."[4]

Nor did Bettie confine her efforts to personal parties. At a 1912 Valentine's debutante luncheon held at another home, she drew the place cards for the table, cupids standing atop a heart and taking aim with a bow. The quality is a bit crude and may reflect either haste or the same health problems that affected her hands and also appeared about this time in the records of the Letitia Rosenberg Home.[5]

For the costume parties so popular in Galveston's elite social circles, Alice drew on her aunt's extensive collection of items purchased on her world travels. To a 1912 peasant dance, Alice wore a Bavarian brocade costume of "exquisite colors" that Bettie had brought back from her 1881-1883 sojourn in Europe. It was complemented, according to the newspaper, by "rare old jewels of sapphires, topaz, turquois [sic], diamonds, and pearls [which] are over two hundred years old and have been in the Brown family for many years." And at Mrs. George Sealy's fabulous Japanese bridge party the same year, Alice wore the "handsome" kimono of dark blue satin embroidered with a large white bird, the emblem of good luck, which Bettie had bought in Japan.

That same winter found Moreau Brown home in Galveston from Chicago with daughter Becky, also making her debut.

Alice hosted a dance for her cousin at the Galvez Hotel, and Charles Rhodes Brown also gave her a dinner party. Three years later, Becky would marry her first husband, Basil Thompson of New Orleans, and name her daughter Bettie Brown (born 1915) in honor of her flamboyant aunt.

This was the last Christmas together for the children of James Moreau and Rebecca Stoddart Brown. John Stoddart, whose name is conspicuously absent in accounts of the festivities, would die in 1912 and his brother Moreau in March of 1914, the latter from what is now known as Lou Gehrig's Disease.

## A CHANGE OF FAITH

Only months before Moreau's death, Bettie stunned her staunchly Episcopalian family, mainstays of Galveston's Trinity Church for decades, by converting to Catholicism.

Her earlier feelings toward that faith show a uniform dislike. She had protested when Moreau married the Catholic Louise Grevenberg after the death of his first wife. Becky Brown (Allgeyer), their daughter, wrote bluntly that "Aunt Betty hated my mother and considered her as 'the scum of the earth Catholic.'" Louise's response was to stay away from Galveston, and Bettie, according to Becky, only visited her brother's second family in Chicago once.[6]

Nor did Bettie like her Catholic brother-in-law Thomas Sweeney, but those feelings were no doubt colored by his treatment of Matilda and their children.

Why she chose to convert is a mystery that Bettie apparently never explained to anyone. One clue lies in the fact that her baptism into the Catholic Church was conducted personally by the Monseigneur James Kirwin, rector of St. Mary's Cathedral, and not by one of his assistants.[7] Kirwin was a powerful figure in Galveston, and his conducting the ceremony may simply have been deference to such a high-profile convert as Bettie. But the two had come to know each other while serving on their respective boards of the Home for Homeless Children. Did Bettie learn to understand and to appreciate Catholicism through this contact? Or did she turn to it out of despair, feeling the Episcopal Church had let her down in the many personal trials she had endured since her father's death? Unfortunately, the bare records give no clue to the motives and feelings of the people involved.

That Bettie was interested in Catholicism from an early date, perhaps even despite herself, is evident in the number of rosaries she purchased on her various trips and kept at *Ashton Villa*. Seven of them still survive in the mansion's collection today, ranging in style from simple stained wooden beads to an elaborate example made of mother of pearl.

## THE CONVERT

On November 1, 1913, Bettie was baptized a Catholic at Galveston's Ursuline Convent, rather than at the Cathedral as was customary. The other oddity is that, on her baptismal record, "there is no indication . . . that the baptism was the conditional one given to someone previously baptized in a Protestant church."[8] Several weeks later, on November 27, she was confirmed at a special ceremony[9] by the Right Reverend Nicholas Gallagher, Bishop of Galveston. Still in *Ashton Villa*'s collection is a miniature book entitled *The Following of Christ* and inscribed as given to Bettie on the Feast of the Epiphany in 1914 "from Mother," probably either Eilleen Goggan or Mary Brotherson, her sponsors.

Eilleen (Aileen) Goggan was the widow of John Goggan, a founder of Thomas Goggan & Co. which sold wholesale and retail musical instruments and "Victor talking machines and records." When her husband died, Eilleen took his place as president of the company, which had stores in Galveston,

Houston, San Antonio, Dallas, and Waco. This executive spirit must have given her much in common with Bettie. Eilleen also served on the board of the Letitia Rosenberg Home, further cementing her relationship with Bettie. Of Mary Brotherson, Bettie's second sponsor, research was unable to turn up any information.

Bettie, who had never done anything by halves, took to her new faith with a passion and is said to have remodeled one of the second floor rooms for a chapel. Family members are divided in their memory of where it was located, except that it was close to her bedroom. The wood columns of what was once the sewing room, on the second floor landing between Bettie's room and her parents', bear marks of having been hinged for a door at some point; so it is possible that was the area she used—if she did, indeed, install a chapel—rather than giving up part of her office.

There is also evidence that, at some point, Bettie painted "An Anglican Nun," which stood for many years on an easel in the reception room of the Ursuline Academy, adjacent to the Convent where she was baptized. Unfortunately, it disappeared after hurricane Carla in 1961. Sister Mary Elizabeth Webster's recollection was that it had been given by James Sweeney, C. J.'s son.[10]

## DEATH OF A BROTHER

Bettie stood in great need of her faith when the last of her brothers, Charles Rhodes, killed himself on November 10, 1916.

Charles' first marriage to Estelle Austin had been a happy one, and his children remembered a jolly man who especially loved Christmas and bought decorations for the house at great cost from Houston. So joyous was the Brown home on Christmas morning that the neighborhood children came to visit first thing in the morning, even before opening their own presents.

But Charles' second foray into nuptial bliss, after Estelle's tragic death, was a disaster. His family hated Elizabeth Hunt, a former housekeeper who heartily returned their dislike.

Charles had experienced a varied career before settling down in Galveston as an agent for New York Life Insurance Company. He followed his father on the board of the Galveston Wharf Company, served as vice president of the Texas Salt Fish Importing Company and as a director of the Garten Verein, and was active as a thirty-third degree Scottish Rite Mason.[11] He was well liked by all and prospered in his insurance business.

Nevertheless, Charles did not consider these to be successes. In his brief will, written the day he died, he declared, "My life has been a failure & my wife———." With that, he walked into an enclosed phone booth in his office and shot himself in the head. Surgeons at St. Mary's Infirmary were unable to save him, and the fifty-four-year-old Charles died seven hours after he was carried to the hospital.

His will left everything to his six younger children (oldest daughter Lydia had married Parker Hanna in 1912 and so was already "cared for"). He allowed his wife Elizabeth to continue living in the Dickinson house but stipulated that she was not "to exact of my children any subservance [sic]."[12] Her revenge was to burn many of the family papers and photographs in the house and to tell the children "malicious tales, some totally imaginary, about Aunt Bettie."[13] Perhaps then, like Thomas Sweeney, Elizabeth Brown is responsible for some of the wilder tales that surround Bettie's history.

## MISS ALICE MARRIES

Less than two weeks after her Uncle Charlie died, Alice Sweeney married New Orleans accountant Henry J. Jumonville in the Gold Room of *Ashton Villa*. Despite their mourning, Bettie and Matilda gave their beloved Alice a beautiful day with an orchestra to provide music and the house filled with flowers and ferns. Charles' elder daughter Lydia even painted James Brown's cherished mahogany staircase white for the occasion, to give Alice a grand entrance. Bettie wore black silk and sequins for her brother but defiantly tied her black lace scarf with a turquoise ribbon, her signature color.

Alice's departure for her new home in New Orleans, and C. J.'s move with Guinevere to their own home, left Bettie and Matilda alone with Moreau in the big rambling house on Broadway. And after his tragically early death two years later, *Ashton Villa* would be a lonely place.

## Notes: Chapter Ten

1   *Galveston Daily News*, February 3, 1910.
2   Morris, *op. cit.*, np.
3   *Galveston Daily News*, in scrapbook of Mary Moody, February 11, 1912.
4   Debut diary of Mary Moody, page 130, in the collection of the Moody Mansion and Museum.
5   Page from Mary Moody debut diary, with sample of place card pasted in. Alice may have shared her aunt's artistic talents, for she designed the red, heart-shaped bonbonnieres and "the dainty heart conceits" used at the luncheon.
6   Letter, Becky to Nell, *op. cit.*
7   Records of the Diocese of Galveston-Houston indicate that Bettie's was the one of the few baptisms Kirwin conducted in October and November of 1913.
8   Letter dated February 20, 1996 from Lisa May, Archivist of the Diocese of Galveston-Houston, to the author. Copy of Bettie's baptismal and confirmation record from the Diocese Archives in Houston.
9   Bettie was confirmed with only one other person. According to Lisa May (see note 7), "most parishes hold Confirmation once a year, when all those to be confirmed receive the sacrament at the same time."
10   Letter dated August 25, 1984 to the author.
11   It is interesting, in light of what subsequently happened to *Ashton Villa* after it passed out of the family, that Charles was a drum major in the El Mina Temple Band. (See Chapter 12.)
12   Galveston County Probate Records, Book 63, page 474.
13   Letter from Rebecca Brown Slack Stanly, dated August 6, 1986, to Dr. Joan Seeman Robinson and in the collection of *Ashton Villa*.

# CHAPTER ELEVEN

# The End of an Era

After decades of a vigorous and healthy life, illness must have been the most frustrating challenge of Bettie Brown's life, one that would not bow to her determination.

## "A PITIFUL SIGHT"

Not until February of 1918 did Bettie resign the presidency of the Letitia Rosenberg Home and settle in at *Ashton Villa* as a semi-invalid. Signs of her declining health had been evident for months in the minute books of that organization. But the extreme seriousness of her illness and its advanced stage is made plain from a quite different source: a letter dated October 17, 1917 from Galvestonian Harry Hawley, a friend of the Browns, to his wife in New York City.

Hawley had dropped in at *Ashton Villa* for a casual visit. "Miss Betty is a pitiful sight," he wrote Sarah Hawley, "for she is drawn and shaking constantly, without the use of her right arm and cannot walk or sit down without much aid. . . ."[1]

Later family members believe her health problems began after she fell and broke her leg, and that she eventually became paralyzed. But Hawley's description, when combined with the causes of death listed in mortuary records, indicates the strong probability that Bettie, like her older brother Moreau, suffered from what is now known as Lou Gehrig's Disease. Galveston Health Department files from Bettie's death two years later state that she died from "lateral sclerosis (spinal)" with "inanition" a contributory cause. All those factors added up, say modern physicians, to Lou Gehrig's Disease.

Amyotrophic lateral sclerosis, as it is properly called, is a slowly progressive and debilitating disease that results when the nerves controlling the body's muscles begin to deteriorate within the brain and spinal cord. First evidence of it is a weakness in the hands and arms, hence, the shakiness of Bettie's handwriting beginning several years earlier. Onset usually begins about age fifty-five, and the disease can run in families. Taken all together—the handwriting, Harry Hawley's description of her inability to move without help, the family's assertion about her paralysis, and the official records—these all indicate Lou Gehrig's Disease as the evident cause of her health problems and, eventually, her death.

What's amazing is that she still continued to be a force at the Rosenberg Home for several months after Hawley's letter was written: the indomitable Bettie Brown refused to give in to her body's demands for as long as she could.

The early death of nephew Moreau Sweeney from tuberculosis in 1918 could only have weakened her. His passing left Bettie and Matilda alone in *Ashton Villa* except for the servants. By Thanksgiving of that year Bettie was no longer able to leave her room, and family members and friends such as Harry visited her there. On that holiday, he wrote his wife, he found her "very much worked up" because she had not been able to procure American Beauty roses to send a newly installed Catholic bishop. "All she could get was some crysanthemums [*sic*] and she was not happy about it." Her attention kept wandering back to this vexing problem, Harry wrote; "she has aged much lately and has a deep incessant cough."[2]

Those outside the circle of immediate family and friends apparently knew nothing of her illness. In *Galveston: A History* (1986), David G. McComb wrote of Bettie: "She was known to have had a bronchial cough loud enough to startle the streetcar mules on the street. Amused contemporaries had gathered to witness the plodding animals awaken with a surprised 'hee haw!' and bolt for the turntable two blocks away." This was an unintentionally cruel interpretation of the cough that accompanied Bettie's final illness and to which Harry Hawley referred in his Thanksgiving letter.

As Bettie's condition worsened, it became necessary to hire a live-in nurse to care for her. The 1920 Census lists thirty-five-year-old Margaret Nellins of Louisiana living there as a nurse but does not indicate how long she had been employed.

## PASSING OF MISS BETTIE

Rebecca Ashton Brown died at 3 p.m. on Monday, September 13, 1920, at *Ashton Villa*, the mansion that had been her home for all but four of her sixty-five and a half years. Lou Gehrig's Disease had wasted her body, but it was uremia—kidney failure—from being bedridden for so long that finally killed her.

Her funeral was held the next day in the church of her adopted faith, St. Mary's Cathedral, but she was buried in the Episcopal Cemetery with her parents, grandmother Sarah Stoddart Rhodes and her second husband, and Bettie's nephew Moreau Sweeney. The pallbearers who carried Bettie on her last journey included some of the most important men in Galveston: R. Waverley Smith, J. W. Terry, John Sealy, George Sealy, F. M. Burton, Charles Fowler (who had served with her at both the Letitia Rosenberg Home and Home for Homeless

Children), W. L. Moody Jr., John Hanna, friend Harry Hawley, Thomas Phillips, Charles E. Witherspoon, John Neethe,[3] Boyer Gonzales, W. R. A. Rogers, Ballinger Mills,[4] Sealy Hutchings Sr., George Copley, Dr. A. A. Arnold, and Dr. William Gannon.[5]

## A TRIBUTE FROM PEERS

A few weeks after her death, the two boards of the Letitia Rosenberg Home passed a joint resolution, the original handwritten copy of which is still in the collection of *Ashton Villa*. Not just personal affection and esteem motivated them, the members declared, but "we feel it a sacred duty to perpetuate her memory, as far as we are able to do so, on the records of that Home, to the interests of which she gave the best efforts of her matured years and upon which she lavished with unstinted generosity her thought, her time, her bounty."

During Bettie's fifteen years of service, the resolution continued, "there was not a single hour that she did not willingly and cheerfully work for the needs of this institution, listening to the petitions and administering to the wants of every inmate thereof."

"By an almost unexcelled executive and administrative ability, she added largely to the 'Ball Fund,' that nucleus of capital which it was her untiring effort to increase to such an extent as to make the Home self-supporting; such financial independence always being a cherished dream of hers." In Bettie's death, the boards declared, "the Home has lost a friend who cannot be replaced. Others on these boards may emulate her efforts, some few may equal them; we know that none will excel in her beneficent work."

This document, presented to her "devoted sister" Matilda Sweeney, provides several points of insight about Bettie. She did not embark on full-scale philanthropy and volunteerism until after the 1900 Storm—her "matured years," as the resolution delicately phrases it. Secondly, she did indeed inherit an executive ability and a gift for diplomacy from her father which were so great that both genteel ladies and men of business had to acknowledge and respect them. And Bettie's financial astuteness seems to have been such that she could probably have maintained, if not enlarged, her share of her father's estate, had not her brother John decimated it.

Lastly, the Rosenberg resolution reinforces a view of Bettie Brown quite different from the popular image of her as a spendthrift, pleasure loving, and reckless woman of fashion. She may indeed have been all of those things in her youth. But life changed Bettie, jut as it does most of us. Some cannot change, and life breaks them. But Bettie refused to bow; she learned from her trials and emerged even stronger.

## PASSING THE TORCH

A week after her sister's death, Matilda filed Bettie's will—written a decade earlier, almost to the day—in Galveston County Probate Court. As brief as her father's had been, and clearly modeled after his in her request to have as little court involvement as possible, the will left "all my earthly belongings to my Sister Matilda Ella Brown Sweeney[,] My Estate real & personal, such as my residence and all its contents inside and outside." Matilda, who was to be her executrix without bond, also received Bettie's quarter share of their mother's estate and bonds on deposit at Rosenberg Bank. Bettie closed her will by declaring, "This I do give with love and affection[.] May God bless her [my sister]."[6]

The inventory of her estate lists the following items: a $50 Liberty Bond, seven Galveston Wharf Company bonds, seventy-six shares in that company, ten war savings stamps due to mature in 1923, eighty-seven shares of American Manufacturing Company (inherited from her mother), twenty-four City of

San Antonio sewer bonds, the lots on which *Ashton Villa* stood, and Bettie's interest in the other real estate holdings in her mother' estate. Interestingly, Bettie had also invested in notes she held through the Security Trust Company: five of them worth a total of $14,250. There was also $3,402.37 on deposit at City National Bank (owned by the Moodys).

In addition, the inventory lists "sundry jewelry and household furnishings" but values them at only $5,000. Was Bettie forced to sell some of her fabulous jewelry to cover living costs and health care expenses? Yet Matilda's descendants, when dealing with her estate, found many pieces of Bettie's jewelry. Perhaps Bettie had astutely given them to Matilda or Alice so as to avoid paying inheritance taxes on them.

Bettie's estate also included assets that consisted of four notes totaling nearly $5,000 for monies she had lent C. J. Sweeney, Matilda's son. Since they date from 1916 and 1917, when C. J. was opening a sporting goods store, it seems likely that his Aunt Bettie loaned him the money to get started in business.

The county judge appraised Bettie's estate at $95,265.37, then deducted the value of debts and war bonds to leave a taxable value of $92,337.16. On that, Matilda paid over $2,500 in taxes.[7]

## AN EMPTY HOUSE

Now the gentle "Tillie" was the last of James and Rebecca Brown's children. She packed up many of Bettie's foreign treasures and paintings and donated them to the recently built Rosenberg Library, which stood just behind *Ashton Villa*. Matilda had long devoted herself to church work and taken over Bettie's space on the board of the Letitia Rosenberg Home, but with her sister gone and the house empty, there was not enough to occupy her. So Matilda divided her time between

Galveston and New Orleans, where daughter Alice Jumonville lived. She died there on January 17, 1926 while visiting Alice. C. J. came from Galveston to bring his mother's body home, and he and Alice buried her in the family plot alongside Moreau, her oldest son.[8] Matilda's will bequeathed the house that had been the family home for nearly eighty years to its third generation, her daughter Alice. But Alice was firmly ensconced in New Orleans and had no plans to return to the city of her birth.

For the first time in sixty-seven years, there was no longer a Brown living in *Ashton Villa*.

## Notes: Chapter Eleven

1   Letter in collection of Galveston-Texas History Center, Rosenberg Library.

   Henry Hawley was a partner in the firm of Hawley & Letzerick, forwarding agents and custom brokers, and knew most of Galveston's prominent families. His home was just a block from *Ashton Villa* at 2327 Avenue K.

2   Letter from Harry Hawley to Sarah Hawley dated November 30, 1918, in the collection of Galveston-Texas History Center at Rosenberg Library.

3   John Neethe served on the board of directors of the Rosenberg Home and his wife Esther was on the Board of Lady Managers.

4   Ballinger Mills' daughter-in-law, Jean Mills, would one day chair the governing committee of the *Ashton Villa* House Museum.

5   Bettie's funeral was handled by F. P. Malloy & Son, which still operates in Galveston. Their records show that her funeral cost a relatively modest $212.50, which included a coffin with a grey crepe interior for $140 and five cars to carry family and friends to the cemetery.

6   Galveston County Probate Records, Book 69, pages 683-687.

7   *Ibid.*, Book 70, pages 203-204.

8   Like her sister's, the list of honorary and active pallbearers at Matilda's funeral reads like a who's who of old Galveston, including George Sealy, W. L. Moody Jr., Ballinger Mills, Sealy Hutchings, and R. Lee Kempner.

CHAPTER TWELVE

# Ashton Villa Reborn

With Matilda's death, *Ashton Villa* entered a new era, one dramatically different from the years in which it had been beloved by the Brown family.

## SALE OF THE MANSION

About a year after her mother's death, Alice Sweeney Jumonville sold *Ashton Villa* to the El Mina Shrine Temple of Galveston for their headquarters. Overseeing the house from her own home in New Orleans was not practical for her, and it would not take long for a house standing empty in Galveston's climate to begin deteriorating.

The Shriners placed an electric neon sign on the front porch but did little structurally to the interior of the original house beyond moving one or two walls and shortening the dining room's chandelier. It was on the back of the house that they made the greatest change, demolishing the 1859 brick kitchen and tearing off the back (north) wall of the family dining hall to expand it for a ballroom that would hold 300 people. Only the staircase to the second floor and the huge fireplace surround and mantel piece were retained from the Brown's remodeling.

Now *Ashton Villa* was once more filled with people. Filing cabinets and desks cluttered the Gold Room, site of so many Brown family events. Women from the associated Eastern Star chapter used several bedrooms for sewing while the men tore down the wall separating the east bedrooms and established a billiards parlor. The El Mina Shrine band—of which Charles Rhodes Brown had once been drum major—used the third floor, and the dining room became a lounge. Later, the Shriners closed in the laundry room/breezeway that had connected the house with the stables and installed a kitchen for ballroom functions.

## NEW TIMES

In an eerie echo of the Browns' own hospitality, *Ashton Villa* again became the site for joyful events: De Molay dances in the ballroom, beer and barbeque parties on the lawn. At Christmas, the Shriners decorated the balconies and eaves with lights. And passers-by frequently stopped on the sidewalk to hear a makeshift concert as the band rehearsed, strains of Sousa and Strauss floating out the open windows of the third floor.

These changes to one of Galveston's finest houses were only the beginning, as this entire Broadway neighborhood began a new life. The Rosenberg Library had been the first "commercial" building erected in the midst of what had been homes and churches during *Ashton Villa*'s heyday. The Victorian home of P. J. Willis, adjacent to *Ashton Villa* at 23rd and Broadway was demolished before 1920; over the next few decades after the Shriners moved into the Brown house, a tire store was built on the Willis site,[1] and a Sears & Roebuck store accross the street. Parking lots and convenience stores increasingly marked the sites of what had once been fine homes.

By the 1960s the Shriners were looking at still another change. *Ashton Villa* was no longer big enough for their needs, and members wrestled with possible solutions. Should they sell the house and build elsewhere? Or would it be more practical to tear down the red-brick structure and build on the same site?

## FOCUS OF ATTENTION

In 1934 *Ashton Villa* was carefully surveyed by architects with the Historic American Buildings Survey, a New Deal project of Franklin Roosevelt's that located and documented many of America's historic structures. Howard Barnstone's 1966 book, *The Galveston That Was*, focused new attention on the city's wealth of Victorian buildings; *Ashton Villa* was included and described as the first of Galveston's great nineteenth-century palaces. Three years later, the mansion became one of the first buildings in Texas to be nominated for and accepted to the National Register of Historic Places, operated by the U. S. Department of the Interior.

So when the El Mina Shrine Temple put *Ashton Villa* on the market for $200,000 and declared they would demolish it if it were not sold within three months, many Galveston and Texas preservationists took alarm. The Junior League of Galveston expressed interest in buying the house but could not afford it.

## ENTER GHF

Then a new player entered the game.

The Galveston Historical Foundation (GHF) dated back to 1871; in what proved to be a fine irony, James Moreau Brown was a charter member. After incorporating in 1954, GHF had undertaken the saving of the plantation-style house built by Texas pioneer banker Samuel May Williams in 1839, one of

161

the two oldest structures left in Galveston. In the next decade, the organization rescued from demolition the western half of the historic Hendley Building on The Strand and renovated it for their headquarters.

Now GHF and its president, Robert Nesbitt, urged the Shriners to save *Ashton Villa*. The best they could do, however, was to get the price lowered to $125,000, so the group looked for other solutions.

Working with the city, GHF successfully sought grants from federal and local funds that allowed the city to purchase the mansion in 1970.[2] That entity then entered into a lease arrangement with GHF to operate *Ashton Villa* as a house museum, which it has continued to do for more than twenty years. Restoration began in 1971 and was completed three years later, thanks in large part to interior photographs of the house made in the 1890s and early 1900s and donated by Matilda's son C. J. Sweeney.[3]

Many of the paintings and artifacts Matilda had donated to the Rosenberg Library after Bettie's death were loaned to GHF for permanent display in the mansion, family members donated more, and additional furnishings were purchased. *Ashton Villa* House Museum opened to the public in late July 1974 and has since been toured by hundreds of thousands of people: almost every visitor to Galveston knows the "big brick house on Broadway with the flags out front."[4]

After years of being closed up, the sound of hammers and saws its only music, *Ashton Villa* again became part of Galveston's social scene, hosting an annual Christmas celebration, participating in GHF's May Homes Tour, and staging dozens of other events. Over the past two decades, the Shriners' ballroom has been the site of countless weddings and parties, as has the Gold Room, a favorite photo location for brides in their wedding finery.

Modern visitors to the mansion enjoy a tour narrated by trained docents, who tell them of the architectural history of the house and of its inhabitants. The wealth and luxury that the Browns enjoyed seems like a fairy tale to most guests.

## MISS BETTIE LIVES AGAIN

But far and away, the favorite personality for visitors is that of Miss Bettie.

No detail of her adventurous life is too insignificant, no story too outrageous to believe about such an outrageous woman. Female visitors sympathize with her desire to have her own way—and envy the wealth that let her do so—while men shake their heads, torn between admiration for such a woman and a certain shrinking fear that their own daughters will grow up to be like Bettie. As *Ashton Villa's* first administrator, Judy D. Schiebel, would have put it, Bettie knocks their socks off.

Visitors drink in the stories and stare at the photographs of Miss Rebecca Ashton Brown in her finery, but how many actually leave *Ashton Villa* with a true understanding of this complex woman?

Bettie is easily seen on a surface level. She was the party-going, globe-trotting, money-spending symbol of America's "Gilded Age" personified. If the late nineteenth century had had an "image," as the 1920s does with the flapper, Bettie would have been the model. But as with most of us, there were many layers to her.

There was the loving and dutiful daughter, who enjoyed an admirable closeness with her father and may, perhaps, have subjugated a desire for a different life in order to care for her parents. There was the astute businesswoman, who was trusted to handle the financial operations of an important Galveston institution.

And there was Aunt Bettie, loving, laughing, teasing, and generous to her bevy of nieces and nephews and, indeed, to most other children who came near her. The philanthropic Bettie, who donated money not for flashy and visible projects, but to plant trees, to treat children to ice cream, or to help an elderly woman to see. And this at a time when her own finances were in disarray through no fault of her own.

There was a strength in Bettie, too, that shows itself in her conversion to Catholicism, an action she must have known would dismay her family but which she did anyway. It appears again when she gamely, stubbornly continued to chair and attend meetings of the Letitia Rosenberg Home far beyond a time when others would have succumbed to the demands of the disease that was ravaging her. It was a strength that showed itself when she gathered together food and clothes and stepped out into the streets of a broken Galveston to help those the great flood had left behind. And even before that, when she supported her sister through a public and humiliating ordeal that most Victorian women would have hidden from.

That strength is commemorated today in the "Steel Oleander" award given annually by the Galveston Historical Foundation to a contemporary Galveston woman who exemplifies Bettie's determination and service to the community.

Hers is the spirit, the feistiness, and the laughter that lights *Ashton Villa*. Without Bettie, it would be just another home of just another wealthy family.

She makes it live, and living was what Bettie Brown was all about.

## Notes: Chapter Twelve

1  This station was itself demolished in 1993. It had been closed for some time and had become an eyesore; its site is slated to become a park-like green space. The irony was that *Ashton Villa* staffers soon realized that the tire store, part of which shared a wall with the mansion's stables, had been supporting the wall. With the removal of the modern building, the stables began to shift and have since required corrective measures.

2  To secure a $50,000 grant from the U. S. Department of Housing and Urban Development, the city had to be the legal owner. Other donors to the purchase were the Moody Foundation ($60,000), established by Brown neighbors and friends Mr. and Mrs. W. L. Moody Jr. and carried on by their daughter Mary Moody Northen; and the Kempner Fund ($10,000), created by members of that longtime Galveston family. The Galveston Historical Foundation gave the remaining $5,000.

   After moving from *Ashton Villa*, the Shriners built a new headquarters, with space for social functions, on The Seawall, where it remains today.

3  Renowned restoration architect Raiford Stripling of San Augustine, Texas, directed the work. He had previously supervised such projects as the restoration of the French Legation in Austin and Mission Esperitu Santo at Goliad. David Warren of Houston's Bayou Bend Museum consulted on the interior furnishings and interpretation.

4  *Ashton Villa* was the Galveston Historical Foundation's first showcase project, which drew much attention from preservationists throughout Texas and the country. In 1982 GHF opened its second major project, the 1877 tall-masted sailing ship *Elissa*, which it had rescued from a Greek shipyard and restored to sailing condition. Built later but in conjunction with the vessel was the Texas Seaport Museum. Then followed a complete restoration

and refurnishing of the *1839 Williams Home*, closed for many years and finally reopened in the winter of 1983-1984. Both properties are owned by GHF itself. In 1984 the Foundation took over from the County of Galveston management of the Galveston County Historical Museum, housed in the Moody's spectacular 1919 City National Bank building. Today GHF also operates the Mardi Gras Museum in Old Galveston Square, and it has a Visitor's Center in the Hendley Building on The Strand. Two important Galveston annual events, Dickens on The Strand in December and the spring Homes Tour, are staged by GHF, as well as regular sails of the *Elissa*.

# APPENDIX A

# History of Galveston, Texas

There are actually three Galvestons: the island, the city located on it, and the modern county (of which Galveston City is the seat), which includes the island, the southern tip of Bolivar Peninsula, and a section on the Texas mainland.

To the east of the island is the Gulf of Mexico; between it and the mainland is West Bay. Together, the east end of Galveston Island and the elongated Bolivar Peninsula are pincers which form the opening of Galveston Bay, which stretches up to modern Houston.

The island is approximately twenty-seven miles long and no more than three miles in width. Low and sandy, it is the northernmost of the barrier islands strung along the Texas coast from there south to Brownsville. The climate is frequently hot and humid, a feature which subjected later European populations to frequent epidemics of yellow fever. Severe storms and hurricanes also lash the island regularly from May through November due to its location on the Gulf of Mexico.

Its native population were Karankawa Indians who occupied the region. Nomadic and thought to have been cannibalistic, the Karankawas were first described by Spanish explorer Cabeza de Vaca on his 1528 Texas journey. Spanish missionaries eventually built several church complexes for the tribe, but most of the Karankawas fled to Mexico after the Texas Revolution.

The Spanish visited Galveston many times over the next three centuries and usually referred to it as Snake Island. In 1785 the Spanish governor of Louisiana, Bernardo de Galvez, ordered the first official survey, and the island was named in his honor. French-born privateer Jean Lafitte used Galveston as his headquarters from 1817 to 1821. Lafitte called it Campeachy and burned the fledgling village to the ground when he fled United States forces.

Jane Long, wife of General James Long, spent the following winter (1821-1822) on the Bolivar Peninsula portion of the modern county. Accompanied only by her maid and small daughter, Jane gave birth there to a second daughter and, in consequence, is frequently called the Mother of Texas.

The first American colonists began to settle on the island in the mid-1820s. When Texas, then part of the Mexican state of Coahuila-Texas, sought and gained its independence in 1835 and 1836, Galveston became an important port and was home base for the naval fleet of the Republic of Texas. During the Runaway Scrape—when thousands of south and central Texans fled General Santa Anna's approaching armies—the government of the new Republic took refuge on Galveston.

Later that year, after victory was achieved at nearby San Jacinto, Canadian developer Michel B. Menard bought the island and organized the Galveston City company, laying out the townsite along the northern, or bayside, harbor. Gail Borden, who would later achieve fame as the inventor of condensed milk, was the first collector of customs when Galveston became a port of entry.

Soon the island was connected to both the Texas mainland and to New Orleans with steam ferries operated by the Morgan Line. Even after the first railway bridge was built to the mainland in 1859 for the Galveston, Houston & Henderson Railroad, the Morgan, Mallory, and other steam lines continued to be an important means of transportation. And over the next two decades, Galveston City grew rapidly with the influx of both Americans and foreigners.

Texas' oldest surviving newspaper, the *Galveston Daily News*, began its operations in 1842; a few years later, the *News* began to publish the *Texas Almanac*, a tradition still continued by its present owners. After the Civil War, the paper was purchased by Colonel A. H. Belo (who had installed the state's first telephone between his home and office). Belo later launched the *Dallas Morning News* as an "offshoot" of the Galveston operation.

In 1845 Texas gave up its sovereignty when its people agreed to be annexed by the United States as the twenty-eighth state. But Galveston continued to reign during the statehood period as Texas' foremost city. The Wharf Company was incorporated in 1854, the Galveston, Houston & Henderson Railroad the previous year. These transportation systems, and the ever-continuing influx of foreign immigrants, pushed the city's population and wealth skyward. By the time the Civil War broke out, Galveston was the state's main port and commercial center and claimed many Texas firsts: first cotton compress (1842), first private bank (1854), first jewelry store (1856), and first gas lights (1856), among them.

Protecting its port facilities was of primary importance to the Confederacy, which Texas joined in 1861. Fortifications and earthworks were built around the city to prevent Federal invasion but were unsuccessful. The United States Navy captured Galveston on October 4, 1862, but it was reclaimed by General John Bankhead "Prince" Magruder on the following New Year's Day. Nearly half of the population fled Galveston as refugees to the mainland during the war. When that conflict ended in 1865, Galveston and Charleston, South Carolina were the only ones remaining open of the South's many ports.

The city then entered on a building frenzy—what one observer called "hurrying times"—as thousands of new residents poured in. The Strand quickly assumed importance as "the Wall Street of the Southwest," and the harbor was designated for development as a deepwater facility by the U. S. Congress in 1889, leading to Galveston's place as one of the largest cotton shipping ports in the world. The city was the home of great wealth, which found expression in the many Victorian "palaces" designed by renowned architect Nicholas Clayton and others. The University of Texas opened the first medical school (still operating today) and the first training school for nurses west of the Mississippi.

The Great Fire of 1885 hardly slowed Galveston down, but the Great Storm of 1900 was another matter. At least 6,000 people died on the island alone in that one terrible night, still the worst natural disaster in U.S. history. Galveston rallied by building a seawall to protect its ocean-front exposure and literally raising the level of the island by pumping in sand and silt. It also established the nation's first commission form of government.

Despite these efforts, Galveston began to lose its position as major port to longtime rival Houston. The 1920s saw the beginning of the "sporting era," when gambling and headlining entertainment meant big business. That ended in 1957 when Texas Rangers closed down the casinos and bordellos for good.

Not until the 1970s did Galveston begin to revive. The rescue and restoration of James Brown's *Ashton Villa* by the Galveston Historical Foundation sparked a firestorm of historic preservation in the city. Today, thanks to these pioneering efforts, Galveston is internationally recognized for its outstanding collection of nineteenth and early twentieth century buildings. Once more the city is filled with exotic color as house after house is painted in the vibrant tones so beloved by Victorian Texans. Millions of visitors come to Galveston every year for a day or a week, enjoying the city's historic neighborhoods, many museums, special events, and beaches.

# APPENDIX B

# Genealogy of the Brown Family

### TABLE 1
### BETTIE'S WELSH ANCESTRY

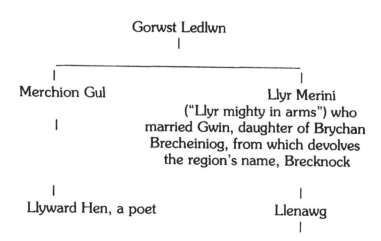

Gorwst Ledlwn

Merchion Gul

Llyr Merini
("Llyr mighty in arms") who
married Gwin, daughter of Brychan
Brecheiniog, from which devolves
the region's name, Brecknock

Llyward Hen, a poet

Llenawg

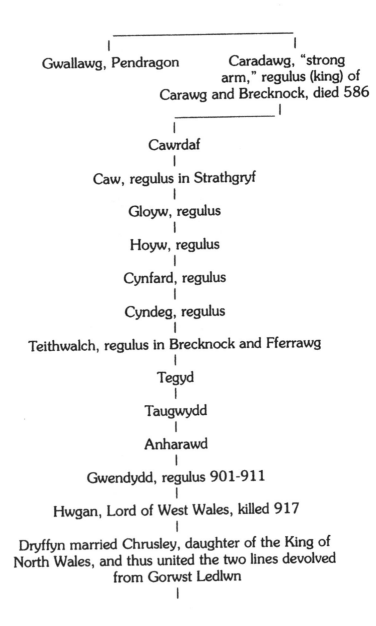

Gwallawg, Pendragon          Caradawg, "strong arm," regulus (king) of Carawg and Brecknock, died 586

Cawrdaf

Caw, regulus in Strathgryf

Gloyw, regulus

Hoyw, regulus

Cynfard, regulus

Cyndeg, regulus

Teithwalch, regulus in Brecknock and Fferrawg

Tegyd

Taugwydd

Anharawd

Gwendydd, regulus 901-911

Hwgan, Lord of West Wales, killed 917

Dryffyn married Chrusley, daughter of the King of North Wales, and thus united the two lines devolved from Gorwst Ledlwn

Maeuard, married Elinor Selyff

|

Bleddyn ap Maenarch, Lord of Brecknock, married Oten,
daughter of Tewdwr Mawr

|

Gwgan (Gurgan), married Gwenllian Gwys

|

Trahaern, Lord of Llangorse, married Joan (Syon),
daughter of Bleddri ap Cadifor

|

Elliyw (Elen), married Rhys Gryg, or Rhys the Lame (?-1233)

|

Howel

|

Rhys ap Howel, who helped capture Edward II in 1326

|

Einion Sais, married Joan, daughter of
Howel ap Meredydd

|

Howel ap Einion Sais, married Llelles

|

Howel Vychan, married Alice, daughter of
Llewellyn ap Howel Hen

|

(1) David ap Howel, Sheriff of Brecknock (no issue)
(2) Llewellyn ap Howel married Matilda, daughter of Ievan

|

(1) Sir Dafyd (David) Gam, who died at Agincourt, 1415
and (2) Howel ap Llywelyn, or Howel Vaughan

|

Gwilym (William) Ddu, "William the Swarthy," married
Margaret, daughter of Jenkin ap Richard Jenkin

|

Howel Ddu, married Maud, daughter of Roger ap Madoc

|

Gwilym ap Howel Ddu, married Catharine, daughter of
Jenkin ap Rhys Tew
|
Howel ap Gwilym (died by 1569), married Margaret,
daughter of William John Havard
|
Thomas ap Howel (in 1569 changed to Powel), married (1)
Sibyl, daughter of Sir William Vaughan and (2) Margaret,
daughter of Walkin Vaughan
|
William Powel, the poet, (?-1620), married Matilda,
daughter of Gruffydd (Griffith ap) Jeffrey
|
Hugh Powel (?-1624), married Elizabeth, daughter of
Thomas Gwyn and descended from Sir David Gam
|
William Powel, a graduate of Jesus College, Oxford
(1597-1637), married Anne Kemeys (ca. 1600-ca. 1644),
daughter of Rhys Kemeys
|
Hugh Powel (1635-1686), Sheriff of Brecknockshire,
married Catharine, daughter of Roger Vaughan
|
Charles Powel (?-1696), married Elizabeth (1656-1729),
daughter of George Gwyn
|
(1) Hugh Powel (1683-1749), who inherited Castle Madoc,
married Margaret, daughter of Walter Thomas
(2) William Powel (?-1754), married Elizabeth ? and
moved to Pennsylvania
(3) Charles Powel
(4) Sybil Powel
(5) Catharine Powel
(6) Anne Powel
(7) Elizabeth Powel, married Rev. John Lloyd

## TABLE 2
## BETTIE'S POWEL AND STODDART ANCESTRY

(= married)
### First Generation
William Powel (1684-1754) = Elizabeth ? - had issue:
- (a) William Powel
- (b) Elizabeth Powel
- (c) Infant, died young

### Second Generation
William Powel (?-1757) = Sarah Mifflin (1718-1795)[1] - had issue:
- (a) William Powel (?-1823) = (1) Anna = (2) Barbara
- (b) Samuel Powel = (1) Elizabeth Moulder - had issue:
  (1) William Powel (1766-1819) = (1) Sarah Gaw
  = (2) Sarah Wetherill from him descends Elizabeth
  Powell (who married Armat Stoddart) and Washington
  Bleddyn Powel, important Philadelphia architect

  Samuel = (2) Elizabeth Coffing
- (c) Isaac Powel = Sarah Rush
- (d) Thomas Powel (died unmarried)
- (e) Joseph Powel
- (f) Rebecca Powel

### Third Generation
Rebecca Powel (1741-1807) = Isaac Ashton (1742-1777) -
had issue:
- (a) Susan Ashton = Joseph Marshall
- (b) Eleanor Ashton = Ezekiel Howell
- (c) Stephen, died in infancy
- (d) Rebecca Ashton

---

1    Sarah married Jacob Lewis in 1759 after her first husband's death.

## Fourth Generation
Rebecca Ashton (1777-1869) = John Stoddart (1777-1869)
- had issue:
- (a) Henry Stoddart (1799-1832)
- (b) Isaac Ashton Stoddart (1801-1854) = Lydia Butler, daughter of Col. Zebulon Butler of Wyoming
- (c) Armat Stoddart (1803-1833) = Elizabeth Powel, daughter of William Powel
- (d) John Stoddart
- (e) Ashton Stoddart I (1806-1812)
- (f) Curwen Stoddart (1809-1890) - in dry goods business with brother Joseph in Philadelphia for 40 years
- (g) Ashton Stoddart II (born and died 1810)
- (h) Rebecca Ann Stoddart (1813-1836)
- (i) Martha Stoddart (1814-1876)
- (j) Joseph Marshall Stoddart (1816-?) = Falmstock (Fahnestock) sisters - see Curwen
- (k) Mary Powel Stoddart (1818-?) = William A. Sterrett
- (l) Eleanor Stoddart (1819-?) = ? Rippinger
- (m) Sarah W. Stoddart (1820-1890)

## Fifth Generation
John Stoddart (1805-1833) = Sarah Warner Moses - had issue:
- (a) Matilda Ella Stoddart = Henry Garlic(k)
- (b) Rebecca Ashton Stoddart

## Sixth Generation
Rebecca Ashton Stoddart = James Moreau Brown - had issue:
- (a) John Stoddart Brown (1848-1912) = Helen de Lespine (1857-1910) - had issue:
    - (1) Rebecca Ashton Brown (Reba) (1874-1950)
      = (1) John T. McClanahan
      = (2) William P. Gaines

(2) Helen de Lespine Brown (1876-1923)
     = (1) George Henderson
     = (2) Van Wyck Thorn
(3) Edgene Stoddart Brown (1881-1920)
     = (1) Eugene Tipps
     = (2) H. G. Henning
(b) Moreau Roberts Brown (1853-1914) = (1) Alice Jane Daughterty - had issue:
  (1) James Moreau Brown (II) (1877-?) = Edna Cullen Moreau = (2) Louise Gravenberg - had issue:
    (1) Rebecca Alice Brown (Rebekah, Becky)
         = (1) Basil Thompson
         = (2) C. L. Ratcliffe
         = (3) Ernest E. Allgeyer
(c) Rebecca Ashton Brown (Miss Bettie) (1855-1920)
(d) Charles Rhodes Brown (1862-1916) = (1) Estelle Austin - had issue:
  (1) Lydia Estelle Brown (1891-1980)
       = Parker D. Hanna
  (2) Rebecca Austin Brown (1893-1979)
       = Torbert Slack
  (3) Matilda Stoddart Brown (1895-1980)
       = Albert C. Crawford
  (4) James Taylor Brown (1896-1969)
       = Ruth Omealy
  (5) Adele Herbert Brown (1900-1985)
       = Arthur W. Ball
  (6) Elizabeth Constance Brown (1903-1976)
       = Byron H. Bartlett
  (7) Estelle Rose Brown (1905-1987)
       = William Alvin Turner

Charles = (2) Elizabeth Hunt (no issue)
(e) Matilda Ella Brown (1865-1925) = Thomas H. Sweeney - had issue:
  (1) Moreau Brown Sweeney (1885-1918)

(2) Charles James Sweeney (C. J.) (1888-?)
= Guinevere Graham
(3) Matilda Alice Sweeney (Alice) (1890-1959)
= Henry Jumonville

## TABLE 3
## BETTIE'S MIFFLIN ANCESTRY

**First Generation**
John Mifflin (1638-1716) = Eleanor ? - had issue:
   (1) John Mifflin

**Second Generation**
John Mifflin (1661-1714) = Elizabeth Hardy (?-1736) - had issue, 9 in all, including:
   (1) Edward Mifflin
   (2) George Mifflin

**Third Generation**
George Mifflin (1688-?) = Esther Cordery (1692-1776) - had issue:
   (1) John Mifflin (1714-1759) = (1) Elizabeth Bagnall - had issue:
      (a) Thomas Mifflin (1744-1800) = ?
      (b) George Mifflin (1746-1785) = Martha F. Morris
   (2) Sarah Mifflin (1718-1795) = (1) William Powel - see Table 2 for issue

# Bibliography

**PUBLISHED SOURCES**

Barnstone, Howard. *The Galveston That Was*. New York: Macmillan Company, 1966.

Bridenbaugh, Carl and Jessica. *Rebels and Gentlemen: Philadelphia in the Age of Franklin*. London: Oxford University Press, 1942, 1968.

Brown, John Henry. *Indian Wars and Pioneers of Texas*. Austin, Texas: L. E. Daniell, Publisher, nd.

Chiarmonte, Paula. *Women Artists in the United States: A Select Bibliography and Resource Guide on the Fine and Decorative Arts, 1750-1986*. Boston: G. K. Hall & Co., 1990.

Davidson, Marshall B. *New York: A Pictorial History*. New York: Charles Scribner's Sons, 1977.

Ericson, Joe E. *Banks and Bankers in Early Texas, 1835-1875*. New Orleans: Polyanthos, Inc., 1976.

*Galveston City Directory*. 1856-1857, 1859-1860, 1866-1867, 1868-1869, 1888-1889, 1890-1891, 1891-1892, 1893-1894, 1895-1896, 1896-1897, 1898, 1899-1900, 1905, 1913, 1916, 1919.

Garraty, John A., editor. *Encyclopedia of American Biography*. New York: Harper & Row, Publishers, 1974.

Grant, Joseph M. and Crum, Lawrence L. *The Development of State-Chartered Banking in Texas, from Predecessor Systems until 1970*. Austin: Bureau of Business Research, University of Texas at Austin, 1978.

Hafertepe, Kenneth. *A History of Ashton Villa: A Family and Its House in Victorian Galveston, Texas*. Austin: Texas State Historical Association, 1991.

Hardy, Dermot H. and Roberts, Major Ingham S. *Historical Review of South-East Texas*. Volume 2. Chicago: Lewis Publishing Company, 1910.

Hayes, Charles W. *Galveston: History of the Island and the City*. Volumes 1-2. Austin: Jenkins Garrett Press, reprinted 1974. Originally published 1879.

*History of Texas, Together with a Biographical History of the Cities of Houston and Galveston*. Chicago: Lewis Publishing Company, 1895.

Hook, J. N. *Family Names: The Origins, Meanings, Mutations, and History of More than 2,800 American Names*. New York: Collier Books.

Howe, Maude Elliott, editor. *Art and Handicraft in the Women's Building of the World's Columbian Exposition, Chicago, 1893*. Paris: Boussod, Valadon & Co., 1893.

Jackson, Joseph. *See Philadelphia: A Visitor's Handbook*. Philadelphia: Joseph A. McGuckin, 1937, 1940, 1953.

Jordan, John W., LL.D., editor. *Colonial Families of Philadelphia*. Volumes 1-2. New York: The Lewis Publishing Company, 1911.

Lehne, Inge and Johnson, Lonnie. *Vienna: The Past in the Present*. Vienna: Osterreichischer Bundesverlag, 1985.

Lester, Paul. *The True Story of the Galveston Flood, as Told by the Survivors*. Philadelphia: American Book and Bible House, 1900.

Linn, John B. and Egle, William H., compilers. *Pennsylvania Marriages Prior to 1790*. Baltimore: Genealogical Publishing Company, Inc., 1979. Originally published 1890.

May, Arthur J. *Vienna in the Age of Franz Josef*. Norman: University of Oklahoma Press, 1966.

Moore, Sylvia, editor. *No Bluebonnets, No Yellow Roses: Essays on Texas Women in the Arts*. New York: Midmarch Arts Press, 1988.

Morgan, William Manning. *Trinity Protestant Episcopal Church, Galveston, Texas,1841-1935: A Memorial History*. Houston: Anson Jones Press, 1954.

Morris, Suzanne. *The Browns of Ashton Villa*. np, 1980.

Naval History Division, Navy Department, compiler. *Civil War Naval Chronology,1861-1865*. Washington, DC: Government Printing Office, 1971.

Nesbitt, Robert A. *The Port of Galveston, 1825-1976*. Galveston: Port of Galveston, 1976.

_____ *Galveston in Retrospect*. Galveston: Port of Galveston, 1978.

_____ *Bob's Galveston Island, Texas Reader*. Revised 1985 edition, n.p.

Nicholas, Thomas. *Annals and Antiquities of the Counties and County Families of Wales*. Baltimore: Genealogical Publishing Company, Inc., 1991. Originally published 1872.

*Palmer's Index to Times Newspaper, London*.

Pickrell, Annie Doom. *Pioneer Women in Texas*. Austin: Jenkins Publishing Company, reprinted 1970.

Rubinstein, Charlotte Streifer. *American Women Artists from Early Indian Times to the Present*. New York: Avon, 1982.

Ruttenber, E. M. and Clark, L. H. *History of Orange County, New York, with Illustrations and Biographical Sketches of Many of its Pioneers and Prominent Men*. Interlaken, New York: Heart of the Lakes Publishing, reprinted 1980.

Southwick, S. B. *Galveston Old and New*. Galveston: Ferdinand Ohlendorf, nd, ca. 1906.

Tobin, Mrs. W. H. "To the Women of Texas." np., nd. In the collection of Center for American History, University of Texas at Austin.

Tolles, Frederick B. *Meeting House and Counting House: The Quaker Merchants of Colonial Philadelphia, 1682-1763*. Chapel Hill: University of North Carolina Press, 1948.

Watson, John F. *Annals of Philadelphia, and Pennsylvania, in the Olden Times*. Volumes 1-3. Philadelphia: Leary, Stuart Co., 1927.

Webb, Walter Prescott, editor-in-chief. *The Handbook of Texas*. Volumes 1-2. Austin: Texas State Historical Association, 1952.

Weimann, Jeanne Madeline. *The Fair Women*. Chicago: Academy Chicago, 1981.

## JOURNALS AND ARTICLES

Axelrod, Bernard. "Galveston: Denver's Deep-Water Port." *Southwestern Historical Quarterly*, October 1966, Volume 70, Number 2.

Moore, Richard and Anderson, Texas. "Gilded Age Archaeology: The *Ashton Villa*." *Archaeology*, May/June 1984, Volume 37 Number 3, pages 44-50.

Phillips, Dr. Edward Hake. "Texas and the World Fairs, 1851-1935." *East Texas Historical Journal*, Volume XXIII, No. 2, 1985.

Seybold, Charlotte Reid. "Resort Attracted Texas Beauty." no attribution, September 18, 1953.

_____ "Interesting Guests at Fountain Springs House." *Waukesha Daily Freeman*, nd.

Smith, Theodore S. "Massawepie." *Adirondack Life Magazine*, May/June, 1980.

"The Family Tree: A Newsletter for Family and Friends of *Ashton Villa*." Summer 1986, Volume 1, Number 2.

Wooster, Ralph. "Wealthy Texans, 1870." *Southwestern Historical Quarterly*, Volume LXXIV, No. 1, July 1970.

## MANUSCRIPT AND OTHER SOURCES

Brochure (photocopy) on Hotel Childwold, circa 1900. Courtesy of The Adirondack Museum, Blue Mountain Lake, New York.

Brochure (photocopy) on Empire Hotel, circa 1905. Courtesy of New York Historical Society.

Brown, Matilda Ella. Diary of. Transcribed by Judy D. Schiebel. Collection of *Ashton Villa* House Museum.

Collections of *Ashton Villa* House Museum, Galveston, Texas.

Collections of the Galveston-Texas History Center, Rosenberg Library, Galveston, Texas:
*Ashton Villa* Collection.
Galveston Health Department: Mortuary Records.
Harry Hawley Collection.
Letitia Rosenberg Home Collection.

Collections of the Moody Mansion and Museum, Galveston, Texas:
Moody, Col. W. L. Excerpts from 1902 Mediterranean-European trip.
Moody, Mary. Excerpts from diary.

Correspondence: letters to author from:
Sandra Roff, New York Historical Society dated January 1984.
Vera L. Kalafarski, Manuscripts Assistant, Mystic Seaport Museum dated February 7, 1984.
Linda J. Evans, Associate Curator of Manuscripts, Chicago Historical Society dated February 8, 1984.
Pamela B. Shadzik, Public Relations, The Waldorf-Astoria Hotel dated February 27, 1984.

Sister Mary Elizabeth Webster, Ursuline Convent,
Galveston, Texas dated August 25, 1984.
Althea H. Huber, Archivist, The Art Institute of Chicago
dated January 11, 1996.
National Association of Women Artists (New York) dated
January, 1996.

Lasker Home for Children. Records. In the collection of The
Children's Crisis Center, Galveston, Texas.

Malloy & Sons Funeral Home, Galveston, Texas. Records.

Phone interviews:
Mrs. T. J. Stanly, Nacogdoches, Texas re Brown family
history.
Dorothy Wolters, Galveston, Texas re history of
Galveston Catholic schools.

Weidler, Beth Anne. "*Ashton Villa* Docent Manual." 1995.

## GOVERNMENT SOURCES

Galveston County, Texas. Records: Probate, Clerk's Office,
District Clerk's Office, Tax rolls, Marriage records.

Internal Revenue Service: Texas. Records. (National
Archives, Fort Worth branch)

U. S. Census, 1850-1920: Galveston County, Texas.
Population Schedule.

_____ 1850-1860: Galveston County, Texas. Slave
Schedule.

_____ 1790-1840: New York State. Population
Schedule

## NEWSPAPERS AND MAGAZINES

*Galveston Daily News*
*New York Times*
*The Opera Glass*
*Saturday Review*

# Index

Made in the USA
Coppell, TX
25 April 2022